HOW TO APPEAL AGAINST A REFUSAL OF PLANNING PERMISSION

I'm particularly pleased that Christian Leigh has produced this book. It is written for non-experts who need to appeal against the refusal of planning permission. Non-professional and 'irregular' appellants struggle to understand and engage with the technical and procedural nuances of this area of planning practice, so Christian's down-to-earth and well-informed guidance is an essential support to ensure that such people can appeal effectively.

Joe Doak, Associate Professor of Urban Planning & Development (1992–2020), Henley Business School, University of Reading

As a solicitor dealing with many aspects of property law, I have found this book extremely useful, allowing me to find a clear, concise and detailed information relating to general planning law.

A very useful book for both those in practice and the general public alike.

Stewart Webb, Consultant Solicitor, Heald Nickinson

These books reflect Christian's professional approach, being clear, concise and very helpful. This step by step approach has been written in a manner that is easy to understand but which also manages to address all the common (and not so common) pitfalls of the Planning Appeals process. Definitely 'Go-To' books.

Charles Doe Architects

Christian Leigh is a planning expert of considerable professional standing and experience, he has assisted my businesses in achieving difficult planning permissions and provided sound advice for over 15 years to help us meaningfully navigate the minefield which has become the demanding planning and Appeal systems in England.

This book sets out clear information and processes which will provide good value to those who buy it, and where Christian has used examples which will relate on a tangible step-by-step basis. An invaluable aid to definitively assist those seeking beneficial planning consents after the negative experience of a planning refusal.

Belinda Simpson, Geoff Beardsley & Partners Architects

Mr Leigh has successfully secured a number of appeals for us and this excellent step by step guide has all the hallmarks of his concise and methodical approach.

Alex Fergusson, AF Architects

We have worked with Christian on a number of planning issues over the years and have always enjoyed his professionalism, pragmatic approach to planning problems and more often than not the result!

Sid Smith, SSPM Project Design Cost Management

Over many years Christian has provided my firm with advice on town planning. This book is an excellent user-friendly guide for small businesses and the public in how to undertake the tricky planning appeals process.

Gary Short, Shorts Group

How to APPEAL against a refusal of planning permission

A STEP BY STEP GUIDE

TO MAKING A PLANNING APPEAL AND WRITING YOUR APPEAL STATEMENT

2020 edition

Christian Leigh MPhil, MRTPI
Chartered Town Planner

ESSENTIAL tips to maximise your chance of **SUCCESS**

www.peculiaritypress.com

ISBN 978-1-912384-11-2

This work first published 2020
by Peculiarity Press, an imprint of Leigh & Glennie Ltd.
The Business Centre, Greys Green Farm, Henley-on-Thames RG 9 4QG, UK.

Contents

Preface

A developer, business or householder who wants to build on their land, or extend a building, or change the use of a building - or whatever the development might be - needs to obtain the crucial grant of planning permission. All applicants hope this will be from the Council, but what happens if the Council refuse planning permission? Or simply fail to make a decision on whether to grant planning permission?

You do not have to just accept the Council's decision. There is a right of appeal to the Government. This allows the case to be looked at with independent eyes, and a new decision made that can overturn the Council's refusal. There are strict procedures to be followed in this route: timetables to be followed, documents that can (and cannot) be submitted, particular information that is expected to accompany an appeal, legislation that must be taken into account, and the possibility of costs being awarded if procedure is not followed properly.

This book covers the law and regulations for England, as there are differences in Wales and Scotland. It explains the procedure and shows how you can make the strongest case to maximise the chance of gaining that essential planning permission. The book will tell you:

- How the appeal system works. What is the appeal system, and who actually decides an appeal?
- Should you appeal? An appeal is not always the best option. What else might you do?
- How do I appeal? The appeal system is highly formalised with deadlines to meet and procedures to follow. If you fail to get this right, you may lose your right of appeal.

- Preparing the appeal statement. Advice on what to include in your key submission that sets out your case at appeal, to maximise your chances and avoid common mistakes.
- The process after lodging the appeal. What happens once you have made the appeal? The lodging of the appeal is only the start. And what can you do if you disagree with the appeal decision?
- Costs. You can apply for costs in an appeal – and have them awarded against you – so you need to know how to avoid the worst happening.

This book does not discuss enforcement appeals or listed building appeals. These are more complex areas that fall under different legislation. This book also does not tell you how to object to planning appeals, but that is covered in my book 'How to object to a planning application or planning appeal'.

About the author

Christian Leigh is a chartered town and country planning consultant, with 25 years' experience working in private planning practice. Over this time his clients have included national housebuilders and development companies, many large and small businesses, as well as local and central Government.

He also works for numerous private clients and householders, as well as providing advice to architects, solicitors, surveyors and other professionals in the industry. This work has involved submitting many successful planning applications and appeals, as well as making representations on behalf of clients objecting to developments.

Christian is, additionally, a visiting lecturer in Planning Law and Practice at the Henley Business School, University of Reading, which is ranked No. 1 in the UK for Land and Property management.

1. What happens when planning permission is refused?

Gaining a planning permission through the appeals process can only happen following the submission of a planning application to the Council (or the local planning authority, or LPA, as properly termed in the appeal process, and will be used in this book).

A planning application will have been made in the normal way to the LPA. It will have been submitted to them and then registered as a valid application. The application will have a unique reference number and a target date for a decision to be made by the LPA. This is usually 8 weeks (though it will be 16 weeks for major applications) and is called the 'statutory period'. The validation, or 'start date' letter received from the LPA will give this information.

The planning application is processed by the LPA in the normal way. They can choose to:

- Approve the planning application
- Approve the planning application, subject to conditions
- Refuse the planning application

There is a right of appeal against the refusal of permission, and also a right of appeal against any of the conditions attached to the grant of permission.

This right of appeal only comes after the decision by the LPA. They must issue a formal Decision Notice granting permission before the right of appeal can be enacted, and the appeal must be lodged within a certain deadline

There is also a right of appeal if the LPA fail to make any decision within the statutory period (the 8 weeks, or 16 weeks as the case may be). This is termed an appeal on the basis of 'non-determination'. It can be made as soon as the statutory period passes, unless you have agreed in writing with the LPA that they can extend the statutory period. The deadlines for lodging appeals, either on the basis of a refusal of planning permission or on non-determination, are very strict, and will be explained later in this book.

The right of appeal only lies with the applicant: the person or company whose name has been put on the planning application form as the applicant. They must be named on the appeal form.

There is no right of appeal for other parties relating to the approval of planning permissions, except for Judicial Review proceedings. The appeal process does, however, have mechanisms for third party involvement (see my book *'How to object to a planning application or planning appeal'* for more details on this).

2. How does the appeal process work?

In this section you will learn:

- What is the formal basis for an appeal?
- Who are the Inspectors who decide the appeal?
- What does the Inspector look at when deciding the appeal?

The appeal is a formal process, made under s78 of the Town and Country Planning Act 1990, and is to the Secretary of State for Housing, Communities and Local Government. It is therefore, in strict legal terms, the Secretary of State who is determining the planning appeal and has the power to overturn the LPA decision. However, in practice, most appeals are determined by an individual Planning Inspector appointed by the Secretary of State. The Inspector is an independent person who has no connection with the LPA.

The appeals system, and the management of the Planning Inspectors, is operated through the Planning Inspectorate. This is an Executive Agency of the Government and they are based in Bristol. Once an appeal is lodged, a Case Officer will be allocated who will be the contact throughout the appeal process.

The actual appeal, though, is determined by the appointed Planning Inspector. It is that independent expert who makes the new decision. Unlike the LPA, there is no committee or panel that sits to determine the case on a majority basis, or any 'signing off' of a decision by a senior manager. The process is technically a tribunal, and the Inspector's decision-making process is quasi-judicial in character. Therefore, at appeal you are looking to make your case to, and persuade, just one person.

There are some procedural differences in appeals, depending on the type of case. But essentially they are all determined in the same way. The appointed Inspector looks at the case afresh. They consider all the evidence presented at the time of the planning application, and the evidence presented with the appeal itself. How you prepare and present this evidence to this one person is therefore very important.

The process is truly independent and impartial. The Inspector will have no ties to the LPA: they do not work for the LPA, nor even live in the area. Inspectors will have many years' experience of the town planning system, but may come from a range of backgrounds, such as town planners, architects, ecologists, surveyors, solicitors. The appeals system is highly regarded amongst professionals for its expertise and independence.

The Inspector, having reviewed the case, will make the new decision on the refused application (or conditions attached to a planning permission, or a non-determined application, if that is the case). They may agree with the case put by any party in the appeal, ie the LPA, the appellant, or any third party who has made submissions, and so may grant planning permission or refuse planning permission. They can refuse permission on different grounds to those put forward by the LPA. Each Inspector exercises their impartial judgement in coming to their decision. Their actions and decisions are, though, governed by the relevant acts of parliament, statutory instruments and case law.

The new decision is binding on all parties. If the Inspector grants permission for the proposed development, the appeal is termed as 'allowed'; if the Inspector decides permission should not be granted then the appeal is 'dismissed'. Whatever the decision is, it can only be challenged through the courts on points of law, not just because one party disagrees with the Inspector's judgement.

KEY POINTS

- The Inspector has no connection with the LPA at all. He or she is truly impartial.
- The professional background of the Inspector could be from anywhere, but will be very experienced in town planning.
- The Inspector considers everything in the case, so can come to a different decision to the LPA, including refusing it on different grounds.
- The new decision from the Inspector is binding.

3. Should you appeal?

In this section you will learn:

- The advantages and disadvantages of appealing.
- Why you might want to carry on discussions with the LPA.

If the appeal process is independent, impartial, fair and can lead to a grant of planning permission that the LPA cannot dispute, why would you not appeal as soon as possible?

One main reason is the delay. Appeals can take a long time. The actual time depends on the procedural route followed (more on that later), but even the simplest householder appeal is likely to take several months. During that time you might be able to undertake negotiations with the LPA about a revised scheme, and have time to submit a new planning application to them and gain planning permission.

A further reason is that you may lose the appeal. This book will help you make your best case at the appeal, but of course success is not guaranteed. The national average for appeals is only around a third successful. The Inspector's appeal decision is binding on all future applications and decisions, so if there is something in the Inspector's dismissed decision that hinders future options for the site, then that may restrict you in the future and the LPA is obliged to take that into account. As mentioned earlier, a dismissed appeal can be on whatever grounds the Inspector judges is relevant, including those put forward by those other than the LPA.

It is important to know that an appeal is not the forum for discussing alternative schemes. The Inspector determines the development that was refused permission by the LPA, and will not be considering any changes to that scheme. Government advice to LPAs is that they should have constructive discussions with an applicant after any refusal of planning permission. So it may well be worthwhile discussing with the LPA how a refused scheme might be modified so a new application can be approved; it could be quicker and more certain than an appeal.

Examples

1 Planning permission has been refused for a two-storey side extension and new garage. The LPA's reasons for refusal related to a window on the side elevation overlooking neighbours, that the extension was close to a mature tree, and due to difficulties in getting a car into the new garage. Rather than going straight for appeal, the householder might first discuss with the LPA if the turning space for the garage could be modified, the extension changed to protect the tree (or more details about construction provided), and decide not to have the window in the side elevation. The LPA may be content with those changes and a new planning application be approved, which is likely to be quicker than an appeal and also not run the risk of a dismissed appeal.

2 A planning application for the change of use of a shop to a restaurant has been refused permission on the grounds that the LPA fear there would be too many customers from the new use, and that there would be smells from the extract system. This is despite the application having specified the hours of use to avoid late nights, and detailing the extract system to be installed. The landowner might be able to offer a further compromise to the LPA - perhaps shorter opening hours, or a different extract system? But if there is no more compromise that could be made, and the applicant wants the independent adjudication of the Planning Inspector, an appeal might be made.

As mentioned at the beginning, there is also the right to appeal against planning conditions attached to the grant of permission. This can potentially be a complex area, and an appeal is not always the best choice to follow. This is discussed separately later.

So think carefully before an appeal. It may well be the way to go, but there could be other options.

KEY POINTS

- **Appeals can be long. Think first about whether there is a compromise or modification that will make the LPA happy to approve a revised application.**
- **Do not use the appeal process to try to negotiate a compromise.**
- **Only appeal if you are confident – as a negative appeal decision can be harmful.**

4. How do I appeal?

In this section you will learn:

- The importance of preparing for the lodging of the appeal.
- A step by step guide on how to complete the appeal form, to avoid mistakes that could make you lose the right to appeal.
- What documents should be included when lodging an appeal, which are commonly forgotten or ignored by many appellants.
- What documents you should not include.

The lodging of an appeal is an important part of the process. There are differences in the types of appeal and strict procedural rules set by the Inspectorate. This means it is essential to understand these rules and what information is required from you when lodging an appeal, otherwise your case will not be presented well, or your appeal may be turned away.

As mentioned earlier, there are some procedural differences in the types of appeal. For instance, householder appeals are always run through an expedited process, which prevents the opportunity to submit information during the course of the appeal. This will be explained further in this section of the book, but what is consistent is that full consideration must be given to how you make your appeal: the process is 'front loaded', so you need to get it right.

STEP 1
BE AWARE OF THE DEADLINES

There are strict deadlines for the submission of an appeal. These cannot be extended, unless there are truly extenuating circumstances. If you are too late, you have lost your right of appeal, so the first step is to be aware of the deadlines.

The deadlines depend on the type of planning application.

Householder application

If the planning application to the LPA was for an extension or works to a single family dwellinghouse (nb that does not include a flat), or development within the curtilage of a dwellinghouse, then the application should be a householder application. A 'prior approval' application for a single-storey rear extension also falls within this category. The validation letter from the Council will inform you if the application was a householder application.

An appeal against a refusal of permission for a householder application must be lodged within 12 weeks from the date of the Decision Notice. Make sure you look at the right date on the Decision Notice. Some LPAs send out their Notice with a covering letter which may be dated later than the Decision Notice. Some Decision Notices have several dates on them such as the date of the planning application, or when amended plans were received. It is the date of refusal on the Notice itself that is relevant.

This means that, for example, a householder application that has been refused permission on 5 May would have to be appealed by 28 July.

Commercial appeals

Certain small-scale applications for works to commercial premises, such as new shopfronts, also have the 12 week deadline for lodging the appeal. Again, the validation letter from the LPA will inform you if the application falls within this category.

Other appeals

All other appeals must be lodged within 6 calendar months of the date of the Decision Notice. This is a simple count of months, not weeks. So, for example, for a Decision Notice dated 5 May an appeal would have to be submitted by 5 November.

Non-determination appeals

An appeal on the grounds of non-determination by the LPA can be submitted as soon as the statutory period has expired, or after expiration of a longer period if that has been agreed in writing between the applicant and the LPA. The appeal must be submitted within 6 months of that date. So, for example, if a planning application had been meant to be determined by the LPA by 5 May but there was no decision by 6 May, an appeal could be lodged any time between 6 May and 5 November. But if you had agreed an extension to the determination period to 18 May then the appeal could not be lodged until 19 May, and then any time until 18 November.

Appeals against planning conditions

If planning permission has been granted subject to conditions, and you do not agree with those conditions, then an appeal can be made to remove or vary any of those conditions. This must be lodged within 6 months of the date of the Decision Notice that grants permission.

STEP 2
GATHER THE REQUIRED INFORMATION

The lodging of an appeal requires the submission of various formal documents, which depends on the procedure being followed:

- the original planning application
- the original site ownership certificate
- the LPA's Decision Notice. If they did not make a decision then you will need a copy of the letter acknowledging the planning application and, if relevant, any agreed extension to the determination date.
- all plans, drawings and documents that were sent to the LPA
- an Ordnance Survey map of the site and local area
- any other documents and evidence that support the appeal which will set out your Statement of Case

STEP 3
REGISTER TO MAKE THE APPEAL

The formal lodging of the appeal is made to the Planning Inspectorate. This is mainly now done online, via the Appeals Casework Portal, at **https://acp.planninginspectorate.gov.uk**

You must set up a user account in order to lodge an appeal online at the Appeals Casework Portal.

There are advantages to the online system as the process has checks to help ensure you submit all the required documentation and so avoid mistakes (but, as will be discussed later, it is not fail-safe). It also means that you have instant confirmation an appeal has been submitted on time, within the timeframes. However, you are still entitled to submit an appeal on paper forms, but be aware these must be requested from the Planning Inspectorate and posted to you, and then posted back, so do not leave that until the last moment. Their address is:

The Planning Inspectorate
Temple Quay House
2 The Square
Temple Quay
Bristol
BS1 6PN

If you chose to make an appeal by post it is recommended you send it by recorded delivery, as if it is received late you will have missed the deadline and your right for appeal.

STEP 4

START THE ONLINE APPEAL PROCESS

The completion of the appeal form and submission of documentation is an extremely important phase of the appeal process. It is often overlooked by appellants as just bureaucracy that is merely shifting around papers. But a comprehensive, neatly prepared and detailed preparation of papers is essential to ensure your appeal gets off to a good start.

The following sections take you through the submission of a new appeal online. There are some small differences in the order of questions for a paper copy submission, but the same information is required in both forms.

The Planning Inspectorate are trialling a new online system for submitting appeals via the Appeals Casework Portal. If your appeal site lies within an LPA in East Sussex, West Sussex or Kent then you must follow a different system for submission. The Portal is clear about this: the Portal will ask you in which county your LPA lies and then direct you to the new system. If this is the case then follow the advice in the Appendix to this book, not what follows.

Click 'Make a New Appeal'

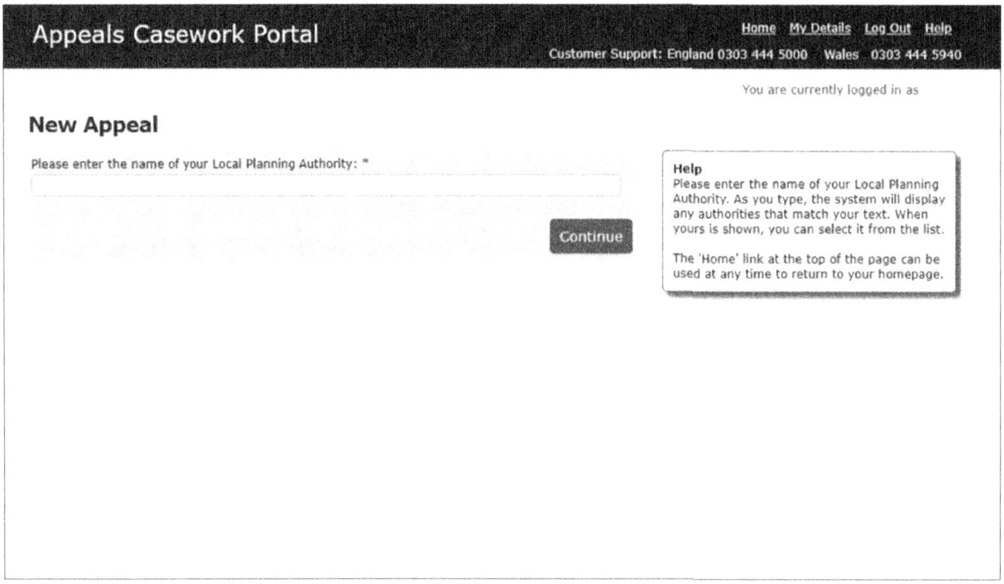

This brings up a new page in which you enter the name of your LPA. Select the correct LPA and press Continue.

'New Appeal': type of appeal

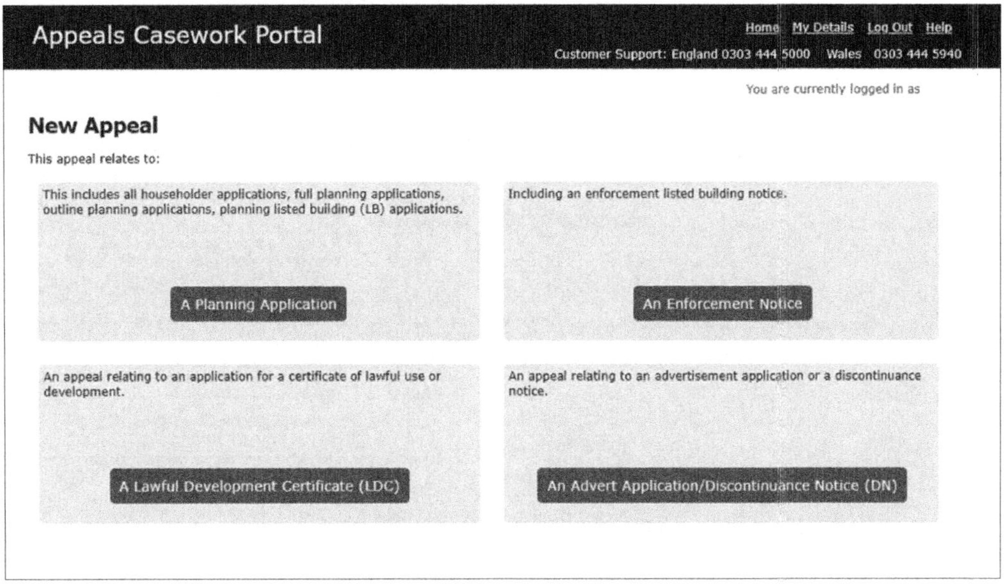

A page of choices appears. This book concerns appeals against the refusal (or non-determination) of planning applications, so choose that button (the other choices on the webpage relate to enforcement matters, lawful development certificates and advertisements)

'New Appeal': planning or listed building

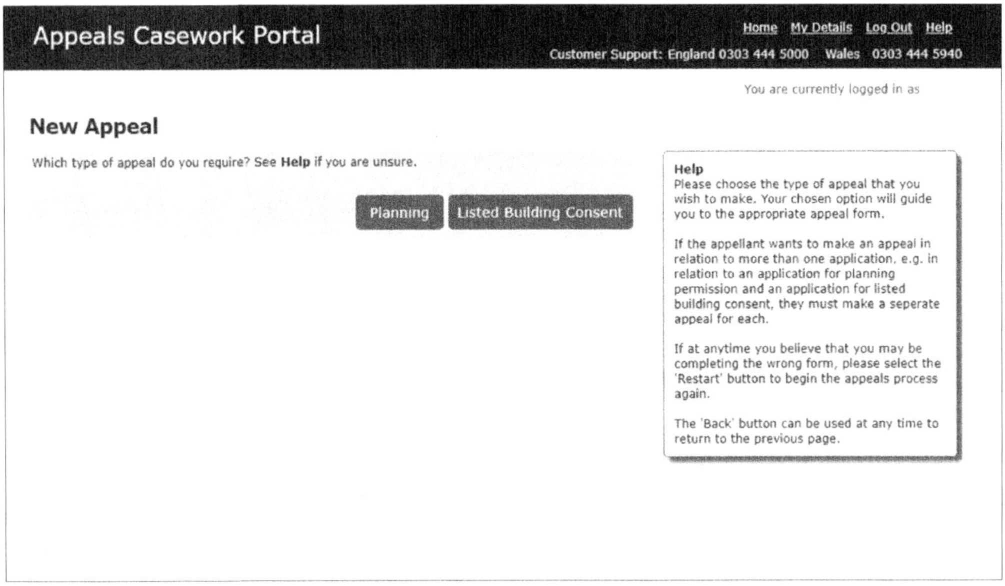

The next page gives an option of Planning or Listed Building Consent. This book does not cover listed building consent applications and appeals and so is assuming the property in question is not listed, in which case click the 'Planning' button.

'New Appeal': single dwellinghouses

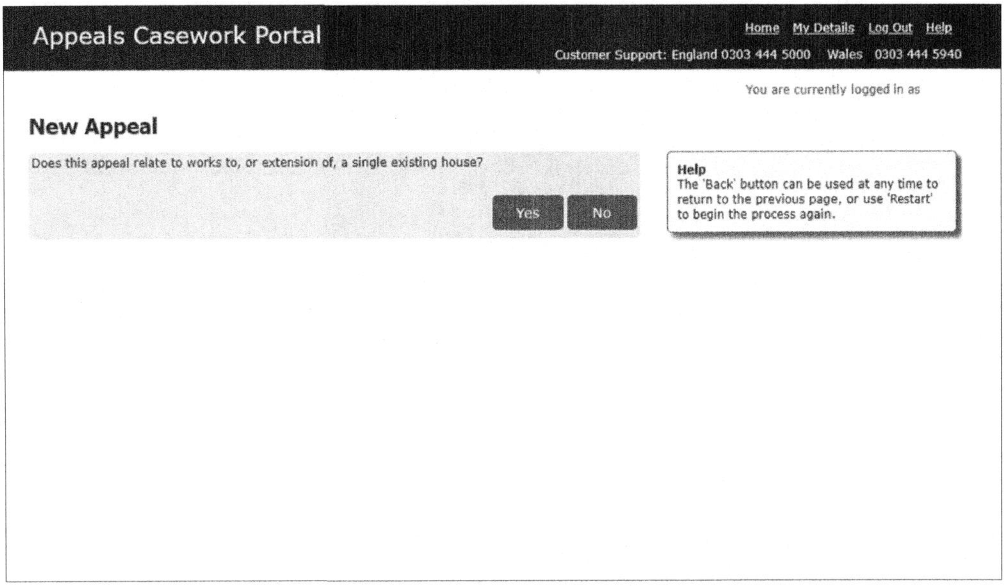

The next page asks if the appeal relates to works to, or extension of, a single existing house. Choose the correct answer: this question is leading you down the route to determine whether the appeal may be the Householder Appeals Service, which is only open to properties that are single family dwellinghouses.

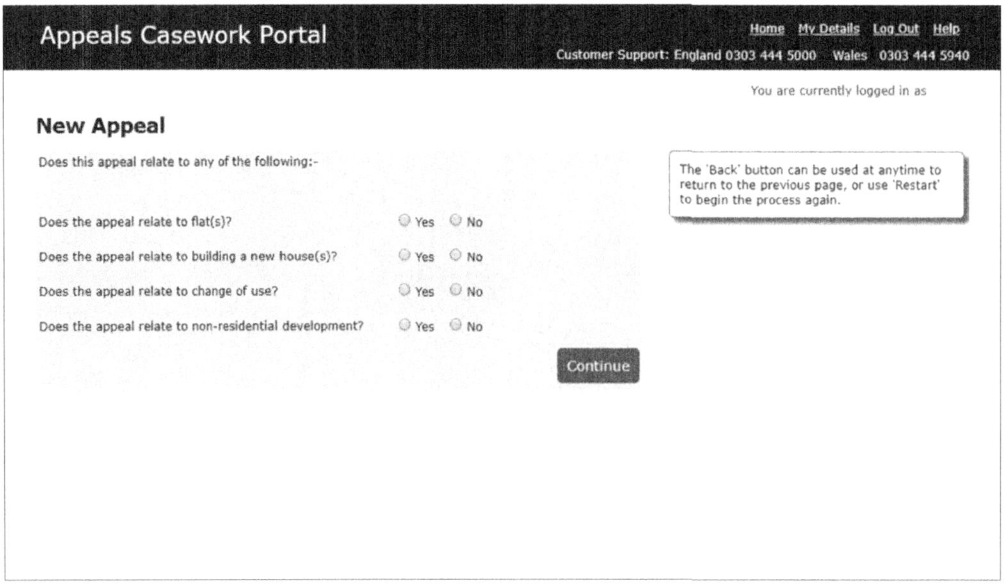

If you click 'yes' to this question, then you are presented with a page that asks you four further question, to double-check that the appeal can be through the Householder Appeals Service (HAS): whether the appeal relates to a flat, or a new-build house, or a change of use, or to non-residential development. It is only if the answer is 'no' to all of these questions then the appeal will be proceeding as a HAS case. Make sure you answer these questions correctly. The online system simply records the choices and then automatically allocates your appeal into the appropriate route for determination. If the Case Officer at the Planning Inspectorate sees, at a later date, that the questions were wrong, and the appeal is in the wrong route, then the appeal will have to change allocation which will lead to delay.

'New Appeal': reason for the appeal

This question gives nine options, one of which must be chosen as the reason for lodging the appeal:

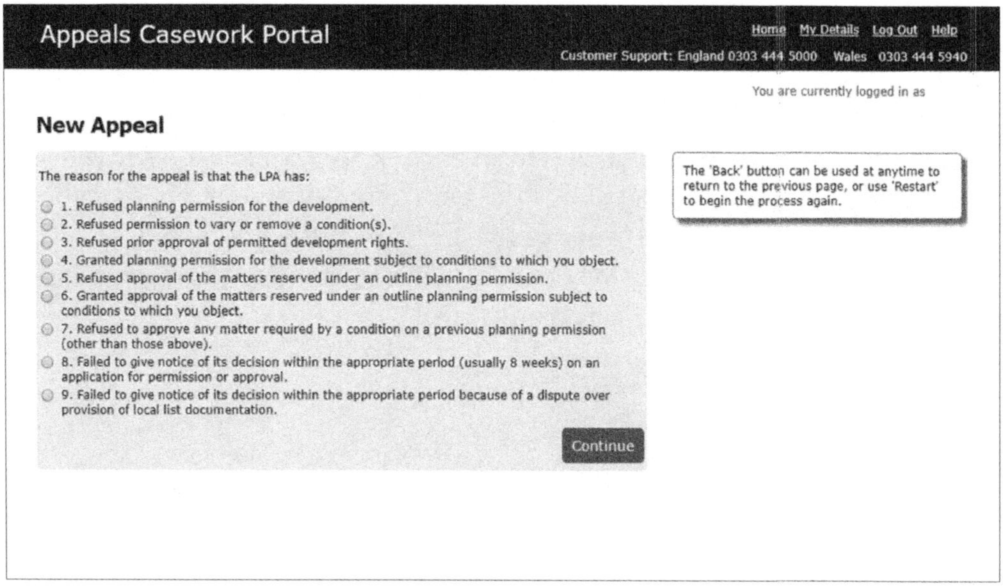

The most likely reason will be Option 1: that the LPA have refused planning permission for the development, which means you have received a formal Decision Notice refusing permission.

If you are appealing on the grounds that the LPA have not determined the planning application within the statutory period then it is Option 8.

Options 2 and 4 relate to appeals against conditions, which is discussed later in this book.

Option 3 relates to a particular type of application that seeks prior approval to take advantage of certain permitted development rights, such as the relaxation of limitations on the depth of rear extensions.

'New Appeal': required form

This page then tells you what type of form you will be completing and is based on your previous questions. The main two choices will be either: 'Householder appeal form' if the appeal property relates to a single family dwellinghouse and there has been a formal Decision Notice refusing planning permission; or in other cases it will be a 'Planning appeal form'.

This page then asks you to give your appeal a name, which is purely for your own reference purposes. When you then click the 'Create appeal form' you are taken straight to the first question of the form. From that point on, though, you can go back to the 'Home' page of your account and the form will be saved as a draft under the 'Awaiting Submission' heading. You can therefore come back to fill in the rest of the form at any time.

STEP 5

COMPLETE THE APPEAL FORM

The online planning appeal form then takes you through a series of questions. Compulsory questions to answer, or compulsory documents to upload, are marked with a red star on the form. After filling in each section, click 'Save and Continue' and the form proceeds to the next page.

The page will not continue if you fail to fill in all the red starred items. If you want to partially complete the page, or skip between sections, then use the drop-down menu in the top corner and you can navigate between pages. That drop-down menu also shows which sections have been completed

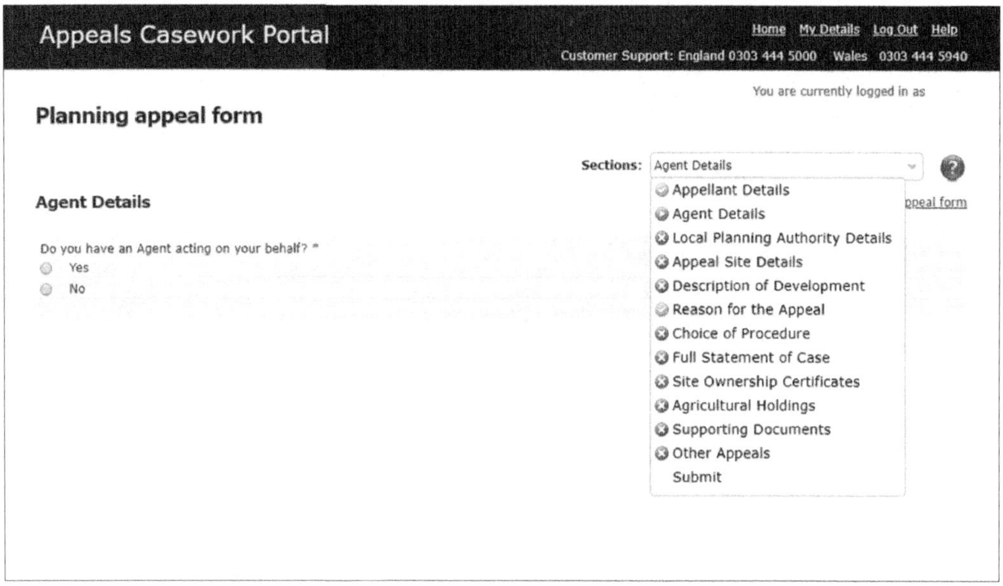

Appellant details

This asks if the person completing the form as the registered Appeals Casework User is the appellant. The appellant's name must be the same as the applicant who was named on the planning application form submitted to the LPA (athough if there is more than one applicant, the appellant can be all of them, or just one). Therefore ensure this question is answered correctly: the right of appeal only lies with the applicant, and if the wrong person tries to claim the right for the appeal it may be invalid.

Agent details

You can employ an agent to assist you in the appeal: a planning consultant, architect, surveyor, or solicitor, for example. If you chose this then all correspondence will go to them. You are not required to use an agent, though. More information on using agents is given later in this book.

Local Planning Authority details

The name of the LPA will have been automatically filled in, from your earlier response. You must then fill in:

- The LPA reference number. This is the planning application reference number, which you will find on the Decision Notice or validation letter you received from the LPA.
- Date of the application. This is the date at the very end of the planning application form the applicant sent to the LPA. Note: it is the date on the application form, not on any validation or start date letter from the LPA. The LPA may give a different date on those letters, but the Planning Inspectorate need to know the date on the application form.
- Did the LPA validate and register your application? This is a simple yes/no question (it does not appear on HAS cases)
- Did the LPA issue a decision? This is another simple yes/no question. If you tick 'yes', then a second box appears asking for the date of the Decision. You must complete this, taking note that you put in the correct date.

Appeal site details

This is the address to which the appeal relates. If it is the same as the appellant's address then clicking 'yes' will automatically fill in the boxes. Otherwise, you will need to enter the details.

The form asks if the appeal site is within the Green Belt, as a simple yes/no question. There is also a question relating to health and safety issues at the site. Obviously, you need to inform the Inspectorate or any particular issues that might be relevant, eg a building site, the need to access high places, hazardous activities on the site, whether the Inspector will need personal safety equipment etc.

Description of development

This question asks if the description of the development has changed from that stated on the application form. When you tick yes or no, a second box pops up asking for you to enter the description.

It is a common misconception that the LPA can alter the description of a proposed development. However, in fact this can only be done if the applicant has agreed to such a change. This is an important matter: you want to be granted planning permission for what you want to build, ie the plans you have submitted, together with the description of the development, comprise that permission.

Therefore, if the LPA has changed the description of the development by the time they issue their Decision Notice, you are not obliged to agree with that description. If you described it in a particular way on the planning application form and you are not content with the LPA's description on their validation letter or their Decision Notice, then you should click 'No' and then enter the description that you set out on the application form. The Inspector should use your description. Having said that, an LPA is able to clarify, or 'tidy up', a description. For instance, if the application form has put an excessively lengthy description of works that are irrelevant, or mistaken, then the LPA may have reworded parts, and an Inspector is likely to do the same.

If you had agreed with the LPA a modified description of the proposal during the course of the planning application you would click 'Yes' in response to this question. This may have been either at validation or perhaps if amendments were made to the proposed development before it was refused permission. In that case, a further box pops up which requires you to attach a copy of any letter that shows the LPA's agreement to that change. This is likely to be the validation letter, or correspondence with the LPA during the course of the application.

This page contains further simple factual questions: the area of the whole appeal site (not just the area of the site you are proposing to develop), the floorspace of the proposed development (the total of all floors) and, other than HAS cases, whether the proposal involves the demolition of non-listed buildings within a conservation area.

Reason for appeal

The list on this page will have been filled out from your earlier questions relating to the preparation of the appeal form, so will be greyed out.

Choice of procedure

There are three choices on the type of procedure, and you can choose which one you would prefer the appeal to follow. These are outlined below, with more detail later in this book.

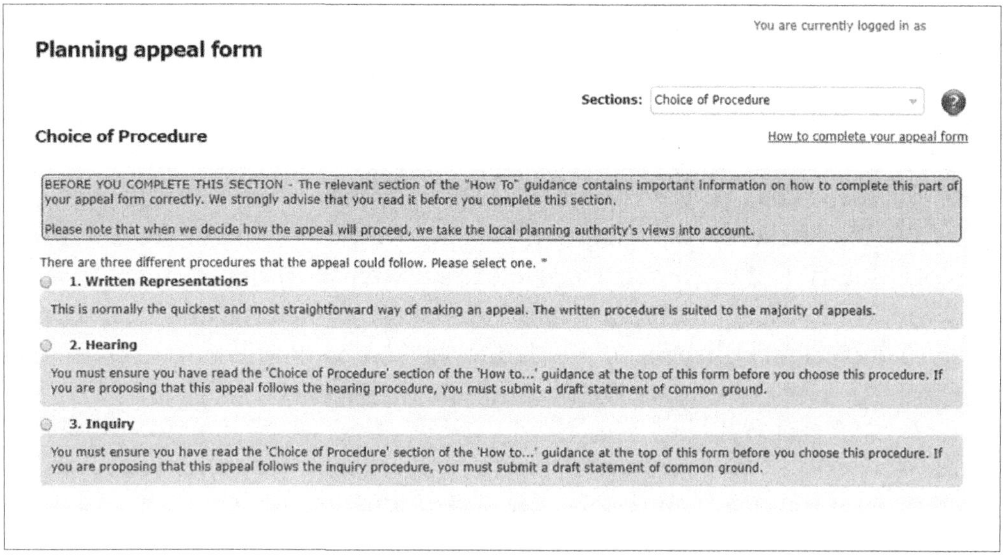

You are currently logged in as

Planning appeal form

Sections: Choice of Procedure

Choice of Procedure

How to complete your appeal form

BEFORE YOU COMPLETE THIS SECTION - The relevant section of the "How To" guidance contains important information on how to complete this part of your appeal form correctly. We strongly advise that you read it before you complete this section.

Please note that when we decide how the appeal will proceed, we take the local planning authority's views into account.

There are three different procedures that the appeal could follow. Please select one. *

1. Written Representations

This is normally the quickest and most straightforward way of making an appeal. The written procedure is suited to the majority of appeals.

2. Hearing

You must ensure you have read the 'Choice of Procedure' section of the 'How to...' guidance at the top of this form before you choose this procedure. If you are proposing that this appeal follows the hearing procedure, you must submit a draft statement of common ground.

3. Inquiry

You must ensure you have read the 'Choice of Procedure' section of the 'How to...' guidance at the top of this form before you choose this procedure. If you are proposing that this appeal follows the inquiry procedure, you must submit a draft statement of common ground.

Written Representations

The Written Representations procedure is the quickest and simplest, and is by far the most common as it is suited to most appeals. The process involves the submission of written submissions by the appellant and the LPA. The Inspector visits the appeal site, but determines the appeal solely on the basis of these written documents. In all appeals except for HAS and CAS appeals, there is a right of reply to these statements for the appellant and LPA, and also the opportunity for third parties, eg neighbours, to write in.

There are advantages in the Written Representations procedure, such as the shorter timeframe and that a well-argued written submission can be very persuasive. But it can lack the opportunity to thoroughly examine the issues through questioning the LPA's refusal, and also the Inspector does not have so wide an interrogative role: they can only read the submissions, and do not ask their own questions.

If you select the Written Representations box then a secondary box appears which asks you whether the appeal site can be seen from public land (Question 1a), and whether it is essential for the Inspector to enter the site (Question 1b). These questions are asked so the Planning Inspectorate can arrange, at a later date, the Inspector's visit to the appeal site. You need to consider this question carefully. The Inspector will need to be able to view everything relevant to the case: the location of the proposed development and anything related to the decision. For example, if the reason for refusal mentioned the effect on trees, then the Inspector will want to see that, or if there is an effect on the windows to nearby houses the Inspector will want to view those.

If all the features can be seen from public land, and the Inspector does not need to enter the site to undertake any measurements, or check other facts, then there is an advantage in ticking 'Yes' to Question 1a and 'No' to Question 1b. Such a site visit is termed an 'Unaccompanied Site Visit' and they are unannounced as the Inspector simply looks at the site from public land. This means the visit may occur more quickly as it is easier for the Planning Inspectorate to schedule unaccompanied visits to Inspectors as they do not need to notify parties, and this means they can sometimes be allocated to Inspectors at short notice if, for instance, another case is cancelled.

However, if you want to be certain that the Inspector sees everything on the site relevant to the case you are making, and that cannot be done from private land, then tick 'No' to Question 1a and 'Yes' to Question 1b. You need the Inspector to understand the whole case, and so he/she needs to view everything. Also, if the Inspector turns up to an unannounced, unaccompanied site visit and realises that there is a need to enter private land then the site visit is likely to be postponed, which will lead to further delay.

Most appeals are, in fact, undertaken with the Inspector entering the land, and there is no issue in selecting this option. Such appeals are termed 'Access Required Site Visits', and a specific appointment is made for the Inspector to visit the site (more on this later).

You may not necessarily have your choice on the site visit as the LPA area also asked for their opinion and the Inspectorate have the final say (more on this later).

Hearings

The Hearing procedure takes longer to determine. The process again involves the exchange of written statements and the opportunity for third parties to comment. However, the appeal will see a Hearing which is an informal forum for discussion led by the Inspector, attended by the appellant, the LPA and any other interested parties. This gives a far greater scope for exploring the issues in the case. The Inspector will always visit the site with an accompanied site visit (so you do not specify a preference on the matter, unlike with the Written Representations procedure choice), and makes the decision based on everything in the written documentation and said at the Hearing and the site visit.

Therefore, the advantages of the Hearing route are that there is a greater chance for the Inspector to be aware of the whole case, through submission at the Hearing and by questioning of the appellant and LPA. The disadvantage, as well as the longer time, is that as you are present at the Hearing, the LPA and the Inspector are likely to ask you questions, and not everyone is good at explaining themselves in person and there is a possibility of 'putting your foot in it' with an unfortunate comment during the Hearing; a well-considered written statement can avoid that.

Again, your preference for a Hearing is not the final say, as the LPA are asked for their opinion and the Inspectorate have the ultimate decision.

Inquiry

The Inquiry procedure takes longer still. It is a highly formalised process. There is the submission of an appeal statement with the lodging of the appeal, but during the course of the appeal the Planning Inspectorate will inform you when a full Proof of Evidence must be submitted to provide a detailed case. This comes before the date of the Public Inquiry itself: a formal event, similar to a court of law in some respects, where the appellant and the LPA usually have legal representation. This process allows for even greater scope to explore and interrogate the issues in the appeal, and to formally question the LPA about their decision. The Inspector will again visit the site, and make the decision based on all the evidence from the Inquiry and written evidence.

The advantages and disadvantages of the Inquiry are similar to a Hearing, but to a greater extent, ie there is even more possibility to examine the issues, but the appellant's evidence will also be thoroughly tested, probably through formal cross-examination. If legal representation is used, there is also a considerable cost. If you select the option for an Inquiry, then the online form will ask you to provide an estimate of the number of professional witnesses you wish to call and how long the evidence will take, and how long the Inquiry will last.

The choice of an Inquiry is again dependent on the views of the LPA and the final decision of the Inspectorate.

What to choose?

The choice of the process is, initially, with the appellant. However, the Planning Inspectorate is not obliged to accept that request, and also the LPA may request a different procedure. The Planning Inspectorate have certain criteria for the procedure; some types of appeal are seen as needing only the simpler processes (the Planning Inspectorate are conscious of the increased resources necessary for the Hearing and Inquiry processes), whilst some types of appeal must always follow the more complex processes (since it is recognised there is a need to interrogate facts). The general guidance is:

- Written Representations appeals are suitable for cases where the grounds of appeal can be understood from written documents, and the issues are not complex with no need for the Inspector to test evidence through questioning. Refusals of planning permission for householder planning applications, or minor commercial developments, are almost certain to proceed through the Written Representations route, and so go into the HAS or CAS procedure.
- Hearings are appropriate where there is a need for the Inspector to test evidence through questioning, or there is considerable local interest, or the status or personal circumstances of the appellant are at issue (usually agricultural workers' dwellings or traveller sites). There should not be any need for formal questioning by an advocate, or evidence to be on oath.
- Inquiries are appropriate where there are complex issues, or a clear need for evidence to be tested through formal questioning by an advocate, or substantial public interest, or evidence to be tested on oath.

Most appeals follow the written procedure. As can be seen from the above list, it is only where cases are more complex that the Planning Inspectorate is likely to agree to a Hearing, and unless the case falls into the specifics examples of an Inquiry then that process is unlikely. If you select the option of a Hearing or an Inquiry, then the online form will ask you to give the reasons for requesting that route.

This means that if you wish to be heard orally, to make your voice heard in front of an Inspector, you must give the Planning Inspectorate very good reason to allocate a Hearing or Inquiry. It is not good enough just to say, in general terms, that you want to be heard, but you will need to explain why there is, for example, particular complexities in the case, or a need for evidence to be examined in detail, or a need to question the LPA about certain matters, or there are particular personal issues to be discussed. The Planning

Inspectorate case officer will want to know why your case fits within the criteria for a Hearing or Inquiry, and it is up to you to give them that detail.

Full Statement of Case

This is where you set out your case for the appeal. The Full Statement of Case must be submitted with the lodging of the appeal, along with any appendices.

How to prepare this document is discussed in detail in the next section of this book. However, there are two further questions on this page of the appeal form (only one in the case of HAS and CAS appeals: there is no Planning Obligation question).

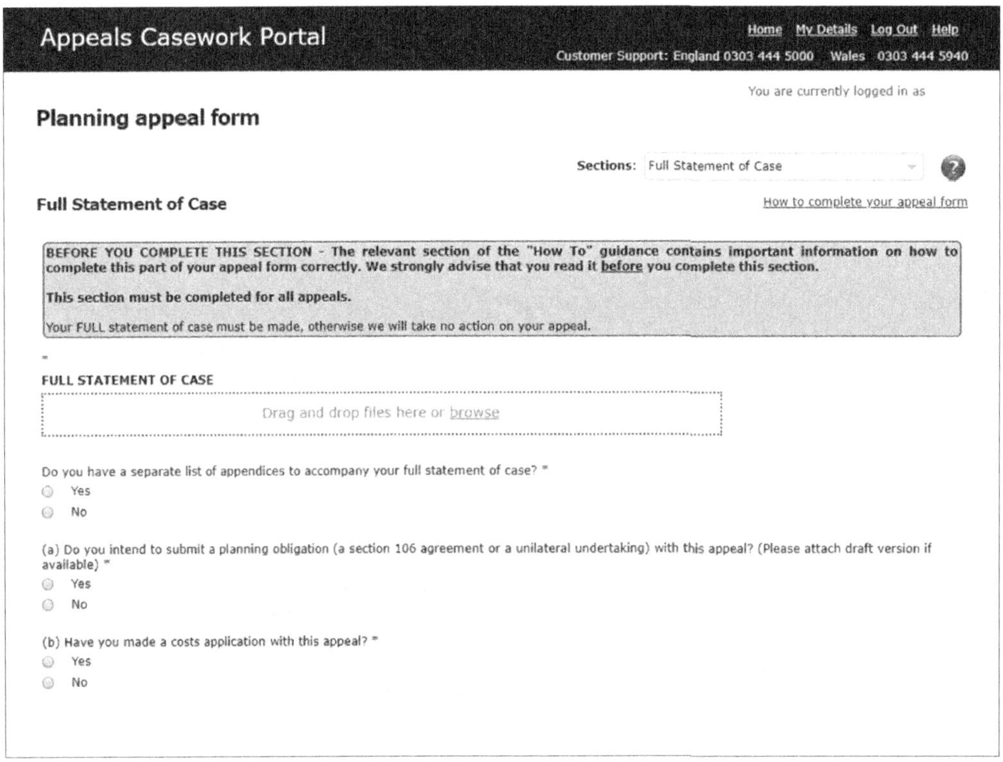

Appeals Casework Portal

Home My Details Log Out Help

Customer Support: England 0303 444 5000 Wales 0303 444 5940

You are currently logged in as

Planning appeal form

Sections: Full Statement of Case

Full Statement of Case

How to complete your appeal form

BEFORE YOU COMPLETE THIS SECTION - The relevant section of the "How To" guidance contains important information on how to complete this part of your appeal form correctly. We strongly advise that you read it before you complete this section.

This section must be completed for all appeals.

Your FULL statement of case must be made, otherwise we will take no action on your appeal.

*

FULL STATEMENT OF CASE

Drag and drop files here or browse

Do you have a separate list of appendices to accompany your full statement of case? *

- Yes
- No

(a) Do you intend to submit a planning obligation (a section 106 agreement or a unilateral undertaking) with this appeal? (Please attach draft version if available) *

- Yes
- No

(b) Have you made a costs application with this appeal? *

- Yes
- No

Item (a): Planning Obligation

Discussions with the LPA during the course of the application may have required you to enter into a legal agreement, or the reasons for refusal set out on the Decision Notice may refer to this. This might be, say, to provide a sum of money for affordable housing, or to limit the use of land in some way.

If you agree with the need to provide a legal agreement then it is very important to realise that a dated, signed and executed legal agreement must be in place before the Inspector issues his/her formal decision. Many appellants are unaware that planning permission cannot be granted 'subject to' a legal agreement.

Not surprisingly, legal agreements can take a long time to produce. You should therefore be undertaking that work at the earliest opportunity, in consultation with a solicitor, to ensure an agreement is completed. Such a document can be submitted with the lodging of the appeal or during the course of the appeal, provided the Inspector and the LPA have sufficient time to review it. If your case involves a legal agreement then you should tick 'Yes' to Item (a) and seek the advice of a solicitor to advise in the preparation and submission of this document.

Item (b): Costs

There is the opportunity for costs to be awarded in planning appeals. It is the only area of the town planning system where there is a punitive costs regime. Costs can be awarded against the LPA, but also against the appellant and third parties. Unreasonable behaviour must be demonstrated, and the intention of the costs regime is to encourage good practice, to ensure that LPAs exercise their duties properly, and that appellants do not pursue unnecessary appeals.

How to apply for costs – and how to avoid having them awarded against you – is discussed later. If you wish to apply for costs then there are time limits for that, but it should be indicated at the lodging of the appeal.

Site Ownership Certificate

When the planning application was made to the LPA, a certificate would have been completed to list the applicant's interest in the land and, if necessary, to list other owners of the land. A similar certificate is submitted at the time of the appeal which states the ownership of the land on the date of lodging the appeal.

The ownership certificate must be completed correctly or else the appeal might be invalid on receipt. Alternatively, at some point in the future, an owner of the land might be able to claim the appeal was falsely made and seek a legal challenge to the decision. You therefore need to fill in these items correctly.

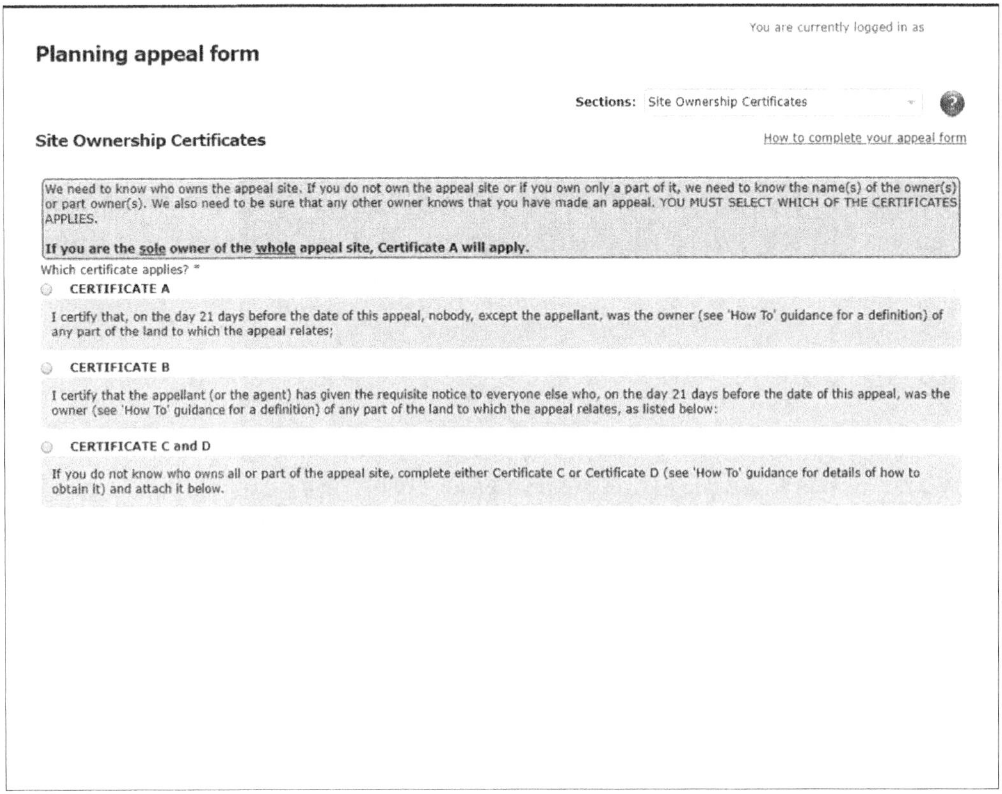

You are currently logged in as

Planning appeal form

Sections: Site Ownership Certificates

Site Ownership Certificates

How to complete your appeal form

We need to know who owns the appeal site. If you do not own the appeal site or if you own only a part of it, we need to know the name(s) of the owner(s) or part owner(s). We also need to be sure that any other owner knows that you have made an appeal. YOU MUST SELECT WHICH OF THE CERTIFICATES APPLIES.

If you are the sole owner of the whole appeal site, Certificate A will apply.

Which certificate applies? *

CERTIFICATE A

I certify that, on the day 21 days before the date of this appeal, nobody, except the appellant, was the owner (see 'How To' guidance for a definition) of any part of the land to which the appeal relates;

CERTIFICATE B

I certify that the appellant (or the agent) has given the requisite notice to everyone else who, on the day 21 days before the date of this appeal, was the owner (see 'How To' guidance for a definition) of any part of the land to which the appeal relates, as listed below:

CERTIFICATE C and D

If you do not know who owns all or part of the appeal site, complete either Certificate C or Certificate D (see 'How To' guidance for details of how to obtain it) and attach it below.

Certificate A

Certificate A is for when the appellant has been the sole owner of any part of the land to which the appeal relates for the 21 days before lodging the appeal. 'Owner' means a person having the freehold interest or a leasehold interest with 7 years or more to run. If you tick this box you then can proceed to the next page of the online form.

Certificate B

Certificate B is if the appellant is not the sole owner of the land for the 21 days before lodging the appeal, and all the other owners of the land are known. If you tick this box then a further box appears.

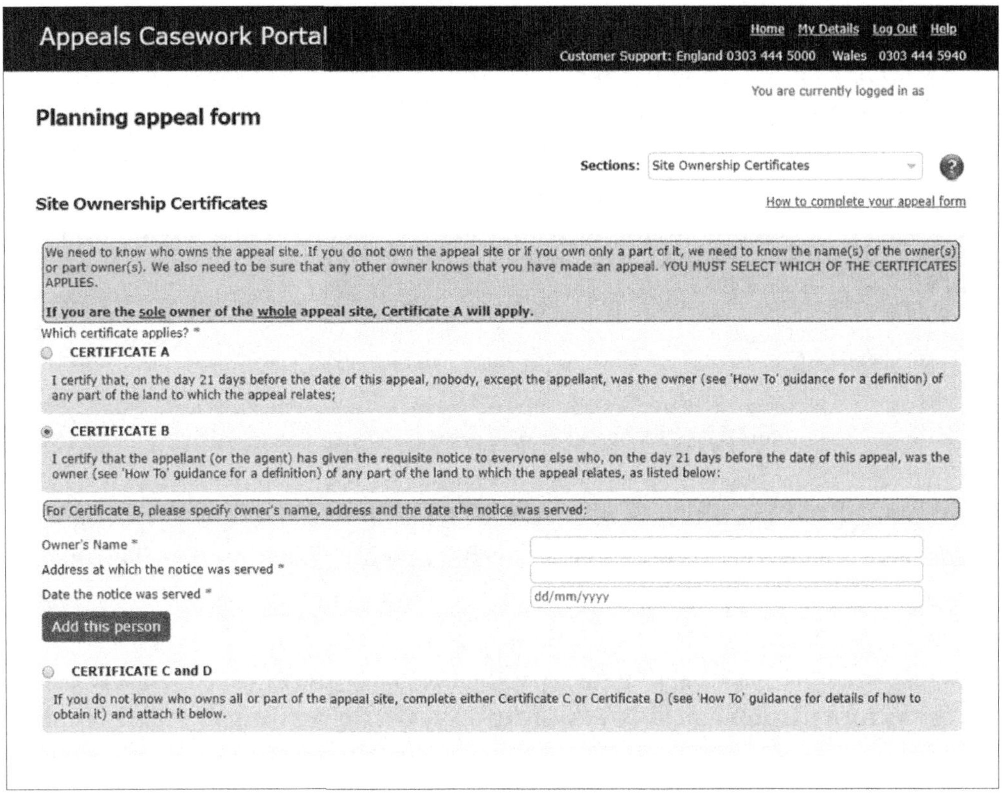

Appeals Casework Portal

Home My Details Log Out Help

Customer Support: England 0303 444 5000 Wales 0303 444 5940

You are currently logged in as

Planning appeal form

Sections: Site Ownership Certificates

Site Ownership Certificates

How to complete your appeal form

We need to know who owns the appeal site. If you do not own the appeal site or if you own only a part of it, we need to know the name(s) of the owner(s) or part owner(s). We also need to be sure that any other owner knows that you have made an appeal. YOU MUST SELECT WHICH OF THE CERTIFICATES APPLIES.

If you are the sole owner of the whole appeal site, Certificate A will apply.

Which certificate applies? *

CERTIFICATE A

I certify that, on the day 21 days before the date of this appeal, nobody, except the appellant, was the owner (see 'How To' guidance for a definition) of any part of the land to which the appeal relates;

CERTIFICATE B

I certify that the appellant (or the agent) has given the requisite notice to everyone else who, on the day 21 days before the date of this appeal, was the owner (see 'How To' guidance for a definition) of any part of the land to which the appeal relates, as listed below:

For Certificate B, please specify owner's name, address and the date the notice was served:

Owner's Name *

Address at which the notice was served *

Date the notice was served * dd/mm/yyyy

Add this person

CERTIFICATE C and D

If you do not know who owns all or part of the appeal site, complete either Certificate C or Certificate D (see 'How To' guidance for details of how to obtain it) and attach it below.

You must enter the details of the owner(s) names and addresses in this box. You must also formally tell those owners that you are lodging the appeal: if you fail to do this, then the appeal could be invalid. You tell these owners by 'serving notice' and there is formal wording for this that must be used. This is included in Appendix 2 of this book, and you can cut and paste it to use. Serving notice should be done in person or by recorded post, and the date you formally serve notice must be included in the correct question on the online form.

Certificate C

Certificate C is used if you know the names and addresses of some, but not all, the owners of the land to which the appeal relates. This requires serving notice on the known owners in the same manner as with Certificate B included in Appendix 2 to this book. However, you must also publish that same notice in a local newspaper (at your own cost). This is so that any other owners may become aware of your intention to appeal. You must send a copy of the published notice to the Planning Inspectorate with your appeal, along with the completed Certificate C, the wording of which can be found online at **https://www.gov.uk/government/publications/planning-appeal-site-ownership-certificates**

Certificate D

Certificate D is used where you do not know the names and addresses of the owners of the land to which the appeal relates. In these circumstances you must publish the same notice as set out in relation to Certificate B in a local newspaper (at your own cost). This is so that any other owners may become aware of your intention to appeal. You must send a copy of the published notice to the Planning Inspectorate with your appeal, along with the completed Certificate D, the wording of which can be found online at **https://www.gov.uk/government/publications/planning-appeal-site-ownership-certificates**

Agricultural holdings

As with the ownership certificate, when the planning application was made to the LPA, a certificate would have been completed declaring whether the application site was an agricultural holding. The Inspector needs to know this information at the time of the lodging of the appeal, so this is a simple question asking whether the appeal site forms part of an agricultural holding.

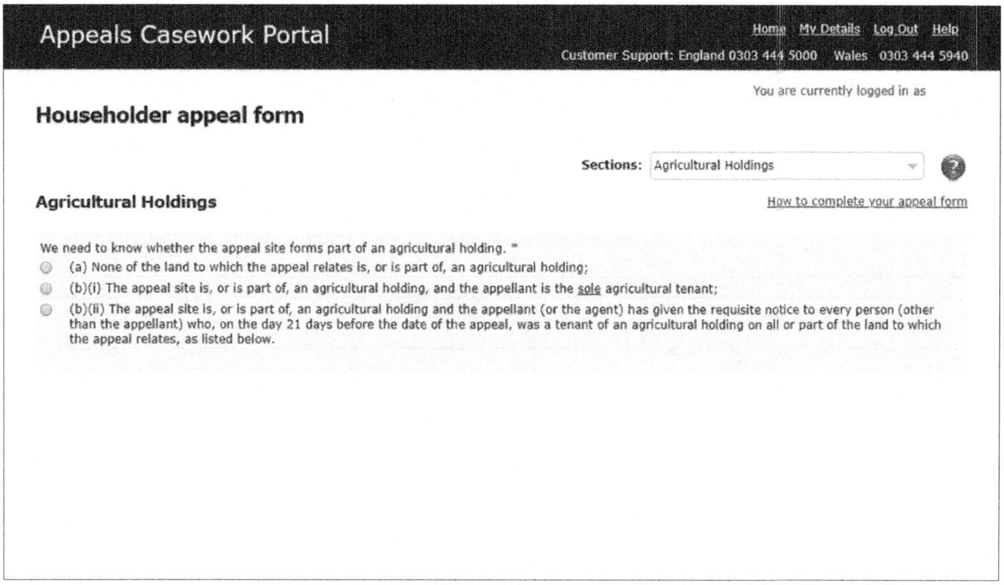

Appeals Casework Portal

Home My Details Log Out Help

Customer Support: England 0303 444 5000 Wales 0303 444 5940

You are currently logged in as

Householder appeal form

Sections: Agricultural Holdings

Agricultural Holdings

How to complete your appeal form

We need to know whether the appeal site forms part of an agricultural holding. *

- (a) None of the land to which the appeal relates is, or is part of, an agricultural holding;
- (b)(i) The appeal site is, or is part of, an agricultural holding, and the appellant is the sole agricultural tenant;
- (b)(ii) The appeal site is, or is part of, an agricultural holding and the appellant (or the agent) has given the requisite notice to every person (other than the appellant) who, on the day 21 days before the date of the appeal, was a tenant of an agricultural holding on all or part of the land to which the appeal relates, as listed below.

If no part of the land is an agricultural holding, then you will tick box (a) and there is nothing else to do.

If the site is an agricultural holding, or part of one, and the appellant is the sole agricultural tenant, then you tick box (b)(i) and there is nothing else to do. However, if there are other agricultural tenants then box (b)(ii) is ticked and you must serve notice, using the same notices and procedure as set out earlier in relation to Certificate B.

Supporting documents

The next question on the appeal form lists the documentation required to create a valid appeal. All this must be received within the 12 week deadline for HAS appeals or 6 month deadline for other appeals, and it must be the correct documentation.

It is therefore extremely important that you check and double check what you are sending. The online appeal submission will only be checking a document is uploaded, not that it is the correct document. That is done at a later date by a Case Officer at the Planning Inspectorate. If that Officer finds you have omitted the correct document, or it is incomplete, then you may miss the deadline. Bear in mind that the check by the Inspectorate on validation may be some days or weeks after you submit the appeal, so if that validation check then falls beyond the 12 week/6 month deadline, you could be out of time. You will have missed your chance to appeal.

The documents are uploaded to the planning portal. It is advisable to send these as pdfs, to ensure no errors when they are received by the Inspectorate. Label the filenames sensibly: you want to make life easy for the Case Officer at the Inspectorate so that your documents reach the Inspector correctly and as clearly as possible. Filenames should have the name of the document (eg 'Decision Notice 5 Jan 2019', or 'Design and Access Statement Oct 2019'). If there is more than one part to a document then label logically (eg 'Appeal Statement Appendix 1 Photographs', or 'Tree survey part 1 of 3'). If you are uploading drawings then label them with the drawing number and paper size too (eg 'Rear elevation 05A at A3 size', or 'site plan 01 at A4 size').

The items you must submit depend on the type of appeal. The online form will tell you which items you need. All appeals require the following:

01. The application form

Again, make sure all pages are submitted. This needs to include the pages that show the ownership certificate that is dated and signed, and the last page of the application form that is dated and signed. Note that if you download a copy of the application form off the LPA's website, some LPAs remove the signature for data protection purposes. The Inspectorate need the full signed and dated copy, so ensure you send them that. A partial form is not a valid form.

02. The Decision Notice

This is the formal refusal of planning permission you received from the LPA. Make sure you submit all the pages: LPAs differ in how they produce these, and some Notices have all the information on one page, whilst others may have a title page and a schedule of reasons for refusal on a second page. A partial Decision Notice is not a complete Notice, and if you fail to send the whole document within the deadline then you may have an invalid appeal.

If you are following a HAS or CAS then these are the only documents you need to send. The appeal form will appear as shown below.

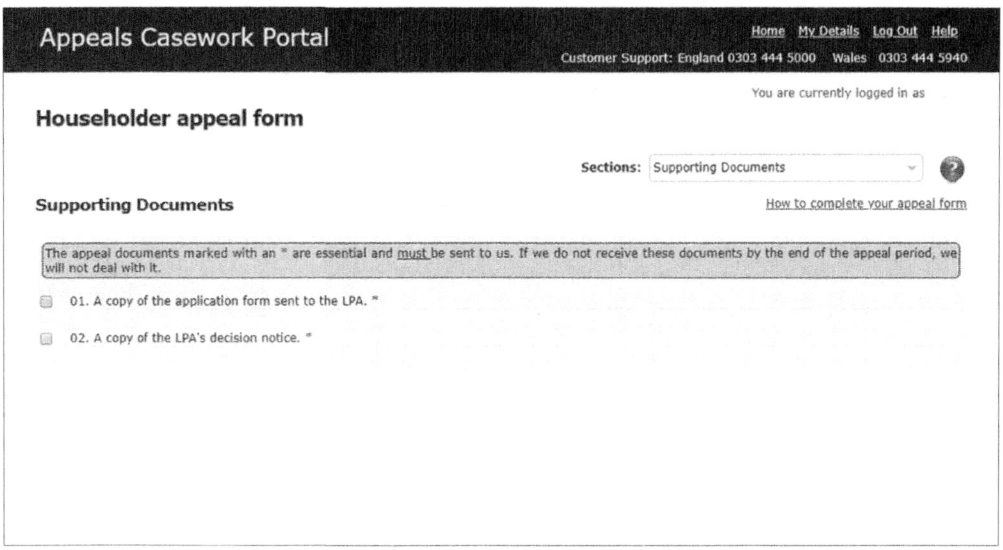

If you are following any other appeal then there is a far longer list of items to be sent to the Inspectorate in addition to the application form and the Decision Notice (listed as items 01 and 03). Not all items are compulsory (only the red starred items must be sent) but certain other items are needed, depending on the appeal.

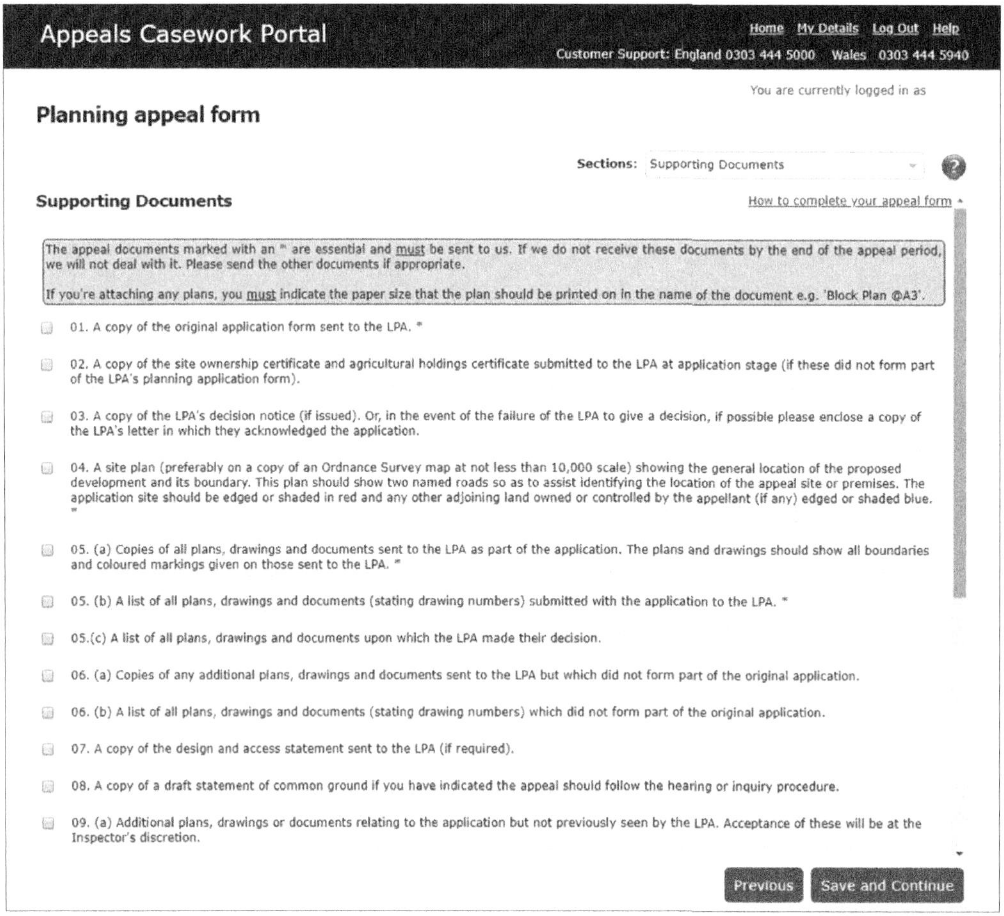

Appeals Casework Portal

Home My Details Log Out Help

Customer Support: England 0303 444 5000 Wales 0303 444 5940

You are currently logged in as

Planning appeal form

Sections: Supporting Documents

Supporting Documents

How to complete your appeal form

The appeal documents marked with an * are essential and must be sent to us. If we do not receive these documents by the end of the appeal period, we will not deal with it. Please send the other documents if appropriate.

If you're attaching any plans, you must indicate the paper size that the plan should be printed on in the name of the document e.g. 'Block Plan @A3'.

- 01. A copy of the original application form sent to the LPA. *
- 02. A copy of the site ownership certificate and agricultural holdings certificate submitted to the LPA at application stage (if these did not form part of the LPA's planning application form).
- 03. A copy of the LPA's decision notice (if issued). Or, in the event of the failure of the LPA to give a decision, if possible please enclose a copy of the LPA's letter in which they acknowledged the application.
- 04. A site plan (preferably on a copy of an Ordnance Survey map at not less than 10,000 scale) showing the general location of the proposed development and its boundary. This plan should show two named roads so as to assist identifying the location of the appeal site or premises. The application site should be edged or shaded in red and any other adjoining land owned or controlled by the appellant (if any) edged or shaded blue. *
- 05. (a) Copies of all plans, drawings and documents sent to the LPA as part of the application. The plans and drawings should show all boundaries and coloured markings given on those sent to the LPA. *
- 05. (b) A list of all plans, drawings and documents (stating drawing numbers) submitted with the application to the LPA. *
- 05.(c) A list of all plans, drawings and documents upon which the LPA made their decision.
- 06. (a) Copies of any additional plans, drawings and documents sent to the LPA but which did not form part of the original application.
- 06. (b) A list of all plans, drawings and documents (stating drawing numbers) which did not form part of the original application.
- 07. A copy of the design and access statement sent to the LPA (if required).
- 08. A copy of a draft statement of common ground if you have indicated the appeal should follow the hearing or inquiry procedure.
- 09. (a) Additional plans, drawings or documents relating to the application but not previously seen by the LPA. Acceptance of these will be at the Inspector's discretion.

Previous Save and Continue

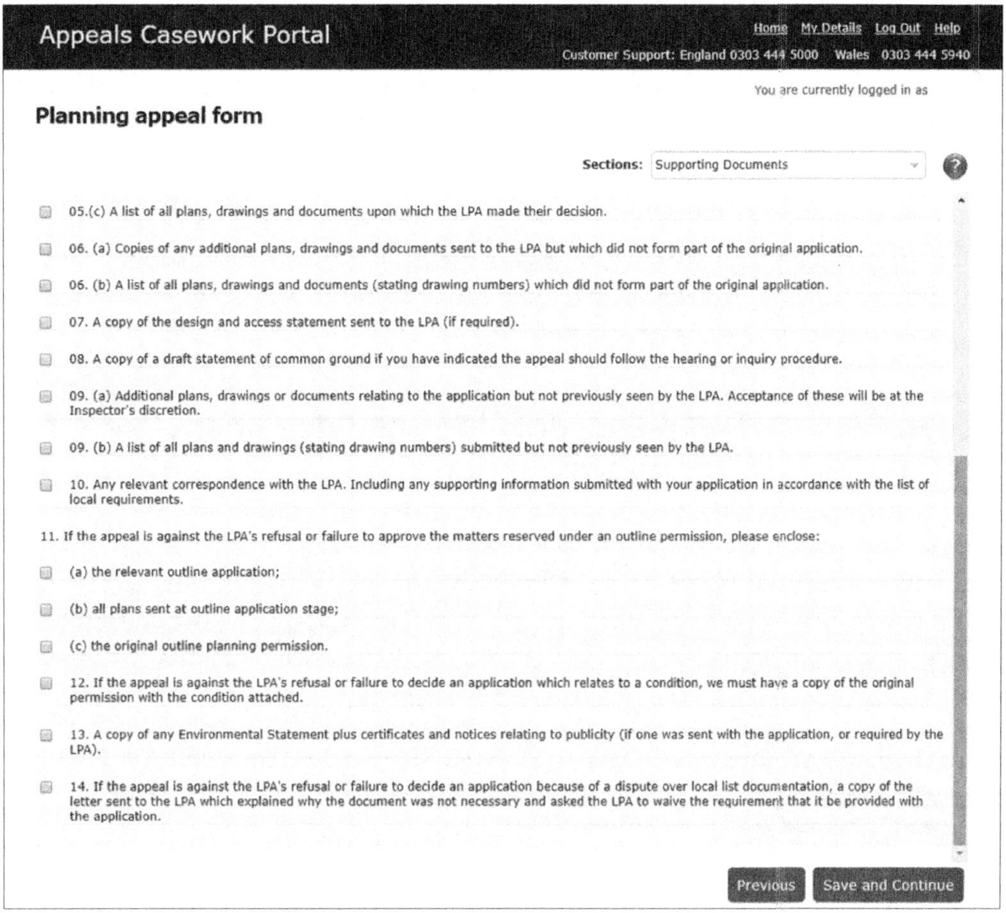

03. The ownership certificate

This is usually part of the planning application form, but may not be. Sometimes there is a need for a new ownership certificate to be submitted during the course of a planning application. Check to see if the planning application form did include the ownership certificate, and if there was a separate certificate at any time then that must be sent.

04. Site plan

This would usually have been part of the application drawings sent to the LPA at the application stage. It outlines the appeal site in red and any adjoining land owned or controlled by the appellant outlined in blue. If the appeal site and area of ownership remains the same as that at the time of the application site plan being produced then it is fine to send the same plan. If there is any difference, or there was not a clear site plan at the time of the application, then you will need to provide a new site plan.

05(a). Copies of all plans, drawings and documents sent to the LPA as part of the application

Unlike HAS and CAS appeals, in other appeals you are required to upload the drawings as refused planning permission by the LPA. This is straightforward, but ensure all are uploaded. Remember to label the file names in a logical way, as set out earlier in this book.

05(b). List of plans, drawings and documents sent to the Council

This is an item commonly overlooked by appellants, or else little attention is paid. The importance is far greater than its name suggests. Unfortunately, errors can be made by everyone: LPAs, the Planning Inspectorate and appellants. Sometimes documents or drawings are not seen by all the parties, or there are errors made in references to drawings. The documents and drawings you sent to the LPA with the planning application still form part of your case at appeal so it is essential that they are seen, eg any supporting Planning Statement, tree survey, flood risk assessment. There can be many documents and you want the Inspector to know what should be read and, as mentioned, unfortunately sometimes these go astray. A clear list should make sure that does not happen.

The List of Drawings therefore needs to clearly set out, in a list, all the drawings and documents that were submitted to the LPA, with a heading to say what the list is. Hopefully, all the drawings you submitted with the planning application had an individual reference.

05(b). Example of a typical list

17 Village Road, London: appeal against refusal of planning permission for rear extension.
List of drawings and documents submitted to LPA:

- 123-01 Proposed block plan
- 123-02 Rev A Proposed elevations
- 123-03 Proposed floor plans
- 123-04 Existing floor plans and elevations
- 123-05 Ordnance Survey red line location plan
- Design & Access Statement, by ABC Architecture, dated 15 February
- Flood Risk Assessment, by MNP Flooding, dated 12 February
- Arboricultural Report, by XYZ Trees, dated 18 February

05(c). A list of plans, drawings and documents upon which the LPA made their decision

Again, this item is often overlooked by appellants and, not being a 'red star' compulsory item, an appeal can be validly made without it being uploaded. However, this list is vitally important. The list for item 05(b) was for those drawings and documents submitted with the planning application. Many items are likely to be the same but there may well have been amendments to a planning application after it was lodged with an LPA, or additional information submitted to address comments by the LPA.

This list for item 05(c) therefore sets out the drawings and documents that were actually refused permission by the Council. Whilst many appellants assume that the LPA will have correctly listed such items on their Decision Notice, unfortunately errors are made by LPAs, or some LPAs simply do not list any documents. You want to make sure the Inspector grants permission for the scheme you intend to build: the Inspector's decision will list the approved drawing numbers, so it is to your advantage to make this procedural matter clear.

05(c). Example of a typical list

5 Village Road, London: appeal against refusal of planning permission for rear extension.
List of drawings and documents upon which the LPA made their decision:

- 123-01 Proposed block plan
- 123-02 Rev B Proposed elevations (revision B submitted 12 April)
- 123-03 Rev A Proposed floor plans (revision A submitted 12 April)
- 123-04 Existing floor plans and elevations
- 123-05 Ordnance Survey red line location plan
- Design & Access Statement, by ABC Architecture, dated 15 February
- Flood Risk Assessment, by MNP Flooding, dated 12 February
- Revised Arboricultural Report, by XYZ Trees, dated 9 April
- Daylight report, by EFJ Lighting Ltd, dated 10 April (additional information submitted)

This example imagines the original proposed elevation and floorplan drawings with the planning application were amended during the LPA's determination process, an amendment was made to the tree report, and additional evidence was submitted regarding daylight.

The clear explanation helps the Case Officer at the Inspectorate, and the appointed Planning Inspector, to understand why the planning application form may have referred to different drawing numbers and documents to those uploaded with the appeal. Using these two lists, with a simple explanation of the different drawings and documents, avoids any questions in the Case Officer's mind – and the Inspector's mind – as to whether you have submitted the correct drawing, and what drawings should be considered. As mentioned before, you need to make things easy for the Case Officer and Inspector.

Of course, if there were no amendments or additional documents submitted during the course of the application then the list will be the same as you prepared for Item 05(b).

06(a). Additional plans, drawings and documents sent to the LPA which did not form part of the original application

These are the drawings and documents that may have been submitted to supplement or amend the application, as you will have listed in response to Item 05(c). If you have made such amendments during the course of the application then the relevant drawings and documents should be uploaded here. Again, remember the advice relating to clear labelling of filenames.

If you did not submit any additional or amended drawings or documents, then you do not need to provide this Item.

06(b) List of plans, drawings and documents sent to the LPA which did not form part of the original application

These documents and plans should have been included on the list you prepared for Item 5(c), since it is a list of those documents and drawings that the LPA determined the application. Provided you prepared a clear and well-explained list for Item 5(c), you can therefore send the same list for this Item.

Again, if you did not submit any additional or amended drawings or documents, then you do not need to provide this Item.

07. A copy of the Design and Access Statement

Certain applications or LPAs will require a Design and Access Statement to be submitted with a planning application. If this was the case then you must upload it here; if you were not required to submit a Design and Access Statement then you do not need to provide it here.

08. Draft Statement of Common Ground

If you intend to follow the Hearing or Inquiry route then you must send this document. This is a written statement containing factual information about the appealed scheme which you consider will not be disputed by the LPA. The intention of the Statement is that time is spent in the Hearing or Inquiry looking at just the differences between the appellant and the LPA. The draft Statement typically covers:

- Description of the site, including agreed dimensions
- Description of the area
- Planning history of the site
- Development plan policies and supplementary planning
- Agreed data or other factors, eg covering matters such as traffic, trees, ecology, etc.

09(a) and 09(b). Plans, drawings and documents relating to the application but not previously seen by the LPA, and a list of those drawings

There is very limited scope to consider revised proposals through the appeal process. It is very important to realise this: the appeal system is not a forum for seeking changes to the refused scheme in an attempt to try to come to a development that is acceptable to all parties. The system does not have a process to consult with the LPA, neighbours and other parties about any amendments to a development, and so accepting changes might be unfair.

This is a common misconception with appellants, who often attempt to submit amended plans or descriptions of development to address the LPA's reasons for refusal, or else set out a desire to negotiate an agreed solution.

Amendments may, exceptionally, be accepted by the Inspector, but in deciding whether or not to accept any changes the principles of fairness to all parties will be taken. This means that the Inspector will consider whether the changes materially alter the nature of the proposed development, and also whether anyone who would normally have been consulted about a development scheme would be prejudiced by the lack of opportunity to comment on the revised plans.

For example, if an application for a two-storey extension has been refused permission by the LPA on the grounds of the height being so tall as to lead to a loss of light to neighbours and being overbearing to their garden, it is unlikely an amended plan that shows a change to the extension will be accepted by the Inspector. The neighbours may still have their opinions about the size of the amended extension, and the appeal process is not a forum to undertake consultation on this.

However, there may be small matters that could be clarified or modified through amended plans. For instance, if an application for an extension to a commercial property had been refused permission by the LPA on the grounds of harm to a tree, overshadowing neighbours, and that the doors to the new bin storage area opened outwards onto a footpath and blocked pedestrians, then you might be able to submit an amended plan showing a revised access to that bin store. This would not overcome all the issues, of course, but could assist in removing one area of contention at appeal and might well be accepted by the Inspector as it is a minor change that is unlikely to be of much dispute, and solves a simple technical issue.

The key message is that only very minor changes might possibly be accepted by the Inspector, so it is best to steer clear of seeking amendments if possible.

10. Any other relevant correspondence with the LPA

There may be additional items that you sent to the LPA during the course of the application, or any correspondence that does not directly show the proposed scheme but you wish the Inspector to see. The online form says this may also include supporting information submitted with the application in accordance with the LPA's list of local requirements. This therefore duplicates the submission made in response to Items 5(a) and 5(b), and so if you have already submitted everything with those Items there is no need to upload again.

11. Approval of reserved matters

If your application to the LPA was seeking the approval of matters that were reserved for future consideration under the terms of an outline planning permission, then you must provide the details of that original outline permission in this section.

Item 11(a) is the outline application itself, ie the application form and any supporting documents.

Item 11(b) is the plans sent at that outline stage and approved by the LPA. It is advisable to send, in addition to this, a list of the approved drawings and any documents, in the same way as you provided in response to Item 05(c).

Although the online appeal form does not ask for such a list, including it will make everything clear to the Case Officer at the Inspectorate, and the Inspector as well, what the documents and drawings relate to, and what exactly were approved by the LPA at the outline stage.

Item 11(c) is the Decision Notice that granted the outline planning permission.

12. Appeals relating to conditions

If you are appealing against a condition attached to a grant of planning permission then you must send the Inspectorate a complete copy of the Decision Notice with that original grant of planning permission.

13. Environmental Statement

If your planning application required the submission of an Environmental Statement then a copy must be sent with the appeal, along with any certificates and notices.

14. Disputes relating to requirements for documentations and validation

An appeal can be made if the LPA refused a planning application on the grounds that you did not provide certain documents set out on their local list of validation, or if they failed to determine an application where you did not provide documentation sought by the LPA. This is a rarely-occurring appeal, but if it is the basis of the appeal then you are required to send the correspondence that relates to the dispute.

Other appeals

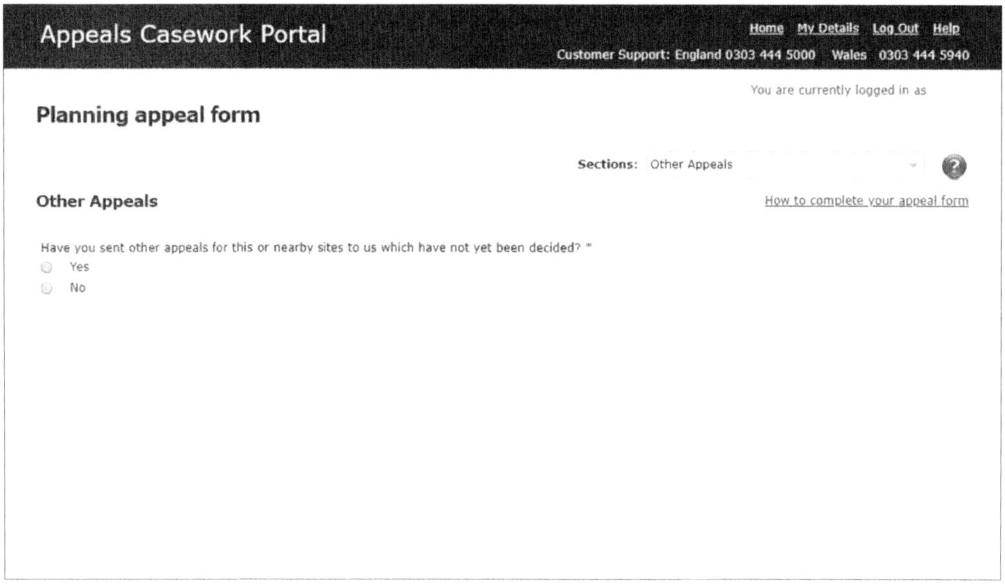

This is a straight-forward question regarding whether there are other appeals already lodged on the appeal site. If you click 'Yes' then you are asked to enter the details.

STEP 6

COMPLETE THE LODGING OF THE APPEAL FORM

When you have completed the preceding question regarding Other Appeals and click 'Save and Continue', you will be taken to a final page to confirm the formal submission.

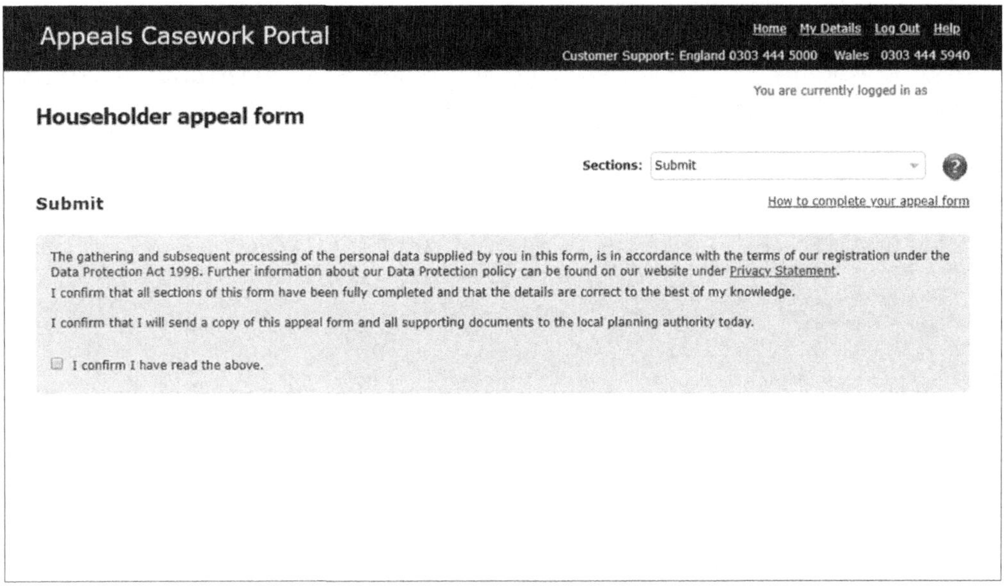

You simply need to tick the box, and then click 'Submit'.

If you have failed to enter the required details on any of the previous pages, or not uploaded the required information, then you will see a page informing you of the errors, and where responses are incomplete. For example, as shown below:

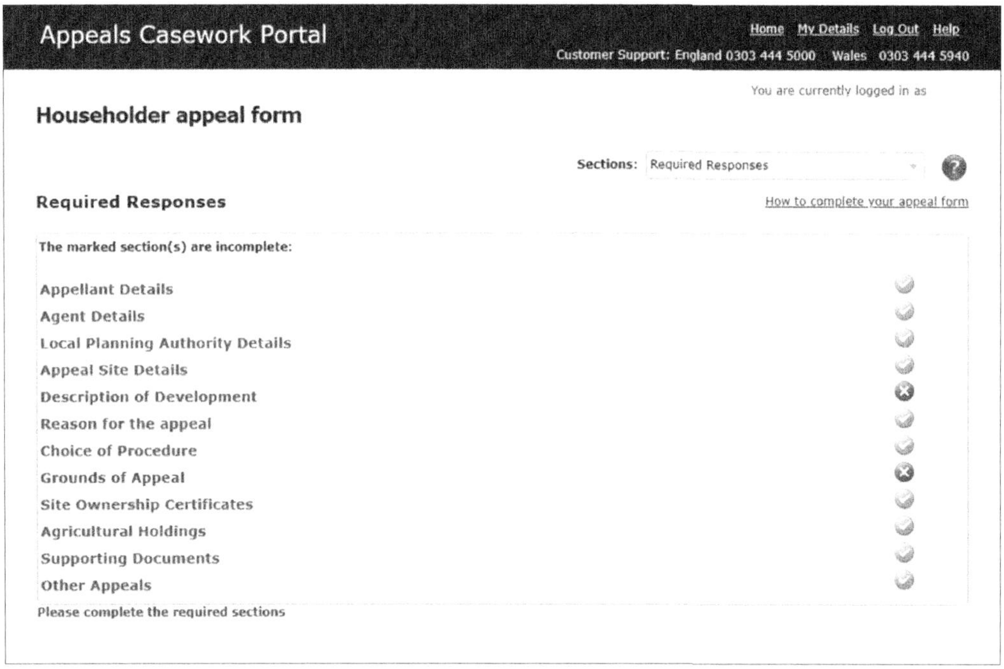

Once you have lodged the appeal to the Planning Inspectorate you will soon receive two emails from the Planning Inspectorate. The first says the appeal has been received, and the second has two pdf attachments which are the appeal form and the personal details form. These will now have a unique reference number on them (starting 'APP'), which is your appeal reference. The top of the forms will also have a time and date stamp that confirms the date you submitted the appeal to the Inspectorate.

STEP 7

SEND A COPY OF THE APPEAL TO THE LPA

You are required to send a copy of the appeal to the LPA straight away. This means both the pdf appeal forms you have received from the Inspectorate and a copy of your Appeal Statement with any supporting documents (see next section of this book). In lodging the appeal you have made a formal declaration that you will do this, and it is an important part of the procedure. No reminder is sent, so it is very important you do this immediately. Each LPA has a different email address, and these can be found at:

www.gov.uk/government/publications/sending-a-copy-of-the-appeal-form-to-the-council

KEY POINTS

- Don't miss the deadlines for an appeal. You will lose your right of appeal if you do!
- Take time to gather all the documents necessary before lodging the appeal: the application documents and your appeal documents. You don't want to be rushing around at the last minute trying to find key items.
- Check and double check the documents you intend to upload are the complete ones. If the Case Officer finds, at a later date, you have missed an item, and you are past the appeal deadline, you may lose your right of appeal.
- Think carefully about the procedure you want to follow: Written Representations, Hearing or Inquiry. You have a choice, but if you want a Hearing or Inquiry you need to provide good reasons to the Inspectorate.
- The Case Officers at the Inspectorate, and the Inspectors themselves, like clear and comprehensive lists of documents. Use lists to set out what drawings and documents you submitted with the planning application, and what drawings and documents were actually refused permission by the LPA.
- You cannot amend a refused scheme through the appeal process or enter into negotiations.
- Don't forget to send a copy of the appeal to the LPA.

5. Preparing the Appeal Statement

In this section you will learn:

- How to target your appeal statement to the issues the Inspector will be looking at.
- The importance of the development plan and the status of planning policies.
- How to respond to neighbours.
- What to avoid in writing your statement.

The principal document an appellant must produce is the Appeal Statement (it is also called the Full Statement of Case, and sometimes called the Grounds of Appeal). This must accompany the submission of any appeal, whether it is following the Written Representations, Hearing or Inquiry procedure. It sets out the case as to why planning permission should be granted and addresses the LPA's reasons for refusal contained in their Decision Notice.

There is no opportunity to add to your Appeal Statement during the appeal process for Written Representations, and only limited opportunities to expand upon your case at Hearings and inquiries. You should therefore only make your appeal when your case has been finalised.

An Appeal Statement needs to cover all the facts and present the arguments to the Inspector, in order to persuade him/her to grant permission. It needs to counter what has been said by the LPA and by third parties. But it should not be too long, or cover irrelevant detail, or to set out irrelevant background information or topics that the Inspector already knows; Inspectors are well-informed and experienced, and want to get to the essence of a case, so do not want unnecessary things to read. The Planning Inspectorate says that, in most cases, an Appeal Statement for a Written Representations appeal should not be longer than 3,000 words. That is only about 6 pages single-spaced in Word, so is not a long document. There is not any absolute limit, though: the Inspectorate will not return documents longer than this word count. But as their guidance is any submission should be clear and concise, you want to be targeted in your Statement.

It is a good idea to include a list of the documentation submitted with the appeal. Your case may be a single document but, as explained later, it may include additional evidence. It may also include an amended drawing or information to address a minor point in the Council's reasons for refusal, though this can only be in the strict limitations set out in the previous chapter. A list may therefore read something like the following:

- Appeal Statement, by J Smith, appellant, dated 18 January
- Supplementary Highways Report, by MNP Traffic Consultants, dated 15 January
- Amended bin store drawing 123-06 Rev B, showing new position of doors to bin store

DESCRIPTION OF THE PROPOSED DEVELOPMENT AND THE PLANNING APPLICATION

It is sensible to provide a general description of what is proposed in the appeal. But it is not necessary to go into great detail about the scheme, or the planning application process, or to repeat the reasons for refusal. The Inspector will be provided with a copy of the Decision Notice, the planning application document, and the Planning Officer's Report or Committee Report produced by the LPA when they determined the application. Repeating all that information in your Appeal Statement is likely to just make your Statement go beyond the 3,000 word target before you even get into the important parts of your case, and divert the Inspector's attention from what you want the focus to be on: why you disagree with the LPA's reasons for refusal.

However, a longer description may be relevant if there is an issue in how the LPA handled the application, eg if they did not take proper account of evidence you submitted during the course of the application, or if they asked you to make amendments. If the appeal is on the grounds of non-determination then it may also be more relevant to describe the process that has occurred: the Inspector may wish to understand why the LPA has not made a decision

Example of what might be included

The appeal relates to a refusal of planning permission for the change of use of the premises from a restaurant to a hot food takeaway, and an extension to the rear of the property.

The application was submitted on 2 February 2019 to the Council with the documents and drawings set out in the List of Drawings, and was refused under Delegated Powers by Decision Notice dated 22 March 2019.

The reasons for refusal raised the following issues:

- The alleged harm to neighbours from the hot food takeaway use arising from noise and fumes.
- The effect of the rear extension on the outlook from neighbouring properties.
- The design of the new extension, and its effect on the character and appearance of the High Street Conservation Area, within which the appeal site lies.

These matters are addressed in this Appeal Statement. Also accompanying the appeal is a Statement on Noise Mitigation, prepared by GH Acoustics.

Example of what might not be included

The appeal relates to a refusal of planning permission for the change of use of the premises from a restaurant to a hot food takeaway, and an extension to the rear of the property.

The application was submitted on 2 February 2019 to the Council and included the following documents:

[a long list of documents and drawings might be put here, which would use up words]

The Council sent a letter on 5 February 2019 asking for an additional plan showing the side elevation. This was sent to the Council on 12 February and the validation letter received on 16 February. The public consultation commenced and on 21 February a telephone conversation with the Planning Officer led to the submission of additional information to show the cooking extract system that would be installed...

[etc; a long description of how the application proceeded is not needed, unless there is some specific reason relevant to the issues at appeal. Your list of drawings that is a required item to be sent with the appeal will set out the documents and drawings]

The Council refused permission under Delegated Powers by Decision Notice dated 22 March 2019. The reasons for refusal are as follows:

1. The proposed use would be harmful to the living conditions of adjoining residents by virtue of the increase in noise arising from the new use, and from odours emitted from the proposed plant and machinery. This would be contrary to Policies EN1 and EN4 of the Anytown Local Plan 2016...

[there is no need to list the reasons for refusal. The Inspector will have a copy of the Decision Notice, and it uses up your word count]

DESCRIPTION OF THE APPEAL SITE AND SURROUNDINGS

It is usually a good idea to describe the appeal site. But the description should only be as relevant as necessary to the issues in the appeal, ie the reasons why the LPA refused permission. The Inspector will be visiting the site, so the idea of the description is to familiarise the Inspector with the issues beforehand. For example, if an application for a rear extension to a house was refused on the grounds of harm to the amenity of the neighbour, then a description of the houses in the area would be relevant, and an overview of how those houses might be positioned relative to each other. But it would not be of interest to the Inspector to be told about what the character of the whole town is like, or if there are nearby bus stops, or if there are shops nearby, etc.

However, if the case involves wider issues then the description should be fuller. An LPA might have refused permission for building two houses on the grounds of harm to neighbouring amenity, effect on trees, the design of the houses, and the remote location of the site. In that instance a far fuller description is needed, referring to everything mentioned above, and in some detail; for instance, where the nearest bus stops, where buses go to, and how often they run; the design of other buildings in close proximity but also further away; the type and condition of trees, etc.

In any description of the site it is helpful to include photographs. Although the Inspector will visit the site, as the Statement is read first it will be useful to gain an impression whilst reading, and as an aide memoire afterwards. Annotation of photographs can be helpful, to show particular features that support the case being made. You should also explain where the photographs are taken from, either in text below the photographs or with a reference map.

Example description

For a single-storey extension to a house, where permission has been refused on the grounds of harm to the neighbour's outlook.

The appeal property is a semi-detached house on the south side of Manchester Road, and is located within the village. The wider area is an estate of housing that all date from the early 1970s, and is a mix of semi-detached and detached housing.

The gardens to the properties are around 20m long, with 1.8m high boundary fences surrounding. The next door property of 12 Manchester Road has an existing rear extension that projects 3.5m from the rear elevation, and is 2.8m to the eaves.

Photographs of the front and rear of the appeal property are attached at Appendix 1 to this Statement.

> *[Note, there is no detailed description of anything other than the appeal property itself, as the issue in this appeal was just the effect of the new extension on the neighbour. Where more specific detail has been given, it relates just to dimensions that might be relevant to issues of outlook, eg the height of fences and the neighbour's extension, the length of the garden]*

Example description

For a new infill house where permission has been refused on the grounds of harm to the character of the area, harm to neighbour's outlook, and amount of parking proposed.

The appeal site is part of the large garden that lies to the side of the detached house of 45 Bristol Road. The site is located within the neighbourhood of Lowerton, which is a suburb of the large town of Anytown. There is a bus stop 50m from the appeal site that serves the main centre of the town with many facilities and centres of employment. Local shops are within 100m from the appeal site.

[It may be relevant in this case to give details about why the site is suitable for new housing as a good location to have dwellings that are close to local services, so specific details should be provided. As the LPA's objection also relates to levels of parking, the availability of public transport and ability to walk to places may also be relevant]

Houses along Bristol Road are mainly detached properties, which stand on plots that are generally of similar dimensions and have frontages to the road that are around 9m wide. No. 45 Bristol Road has a wider plot of around 16m, and so is almost twice the average width of plots in the area. The character of the area then changes to the west, where houses along Bath Road are generally semi-detached and stand on smaller plots. Properties have off-street parking, but car parking is also available on the road and there is a low level of on-street parking. Photographs of the appeal site and wider area are attached at Appendix 1.

[As the issues relate to the character of the wider area, it is relevant to refer to the general appearance of the street and other streets, to show that the creation of a smaller plot is in character. The photographs at the appendix would need to be annotated to show where they are taken.]

The next door property of 47 Bristol Road is situated 2m from the boundary with the appeal site. There is one window on the side elevation facing the appeal site, which is obscure glazed as it serves a bathroom. There is an extension to the rear of No. 47 that projects 4m into the garden, beyond the rear elevation.

[As effect on neighbouring outlook is an issue it is relevant to set out the relationship between the appeal site and the neighbour.]

PLANNING POLICIES

The law states that the decision on whether to grant planning permission must be made in accordance with the development plan, unless material considerations indicate otherwise.

The development plan

This means that planning permission can only be granted by the Inspector if he/she is satisfied that the proposed development accords with planning policies. If the Inspector concludes the development does not accord with those policies, then permission must be refused, unless there are particular circumstances that allow for a departure from those policies.

An Appeal Statement must therefore seek to persuade an Inspector that your proposed development satisfies the relevant policies. This is an element that can be overlooked by appellants. Simply countering the LPA's reasons for refusal with opinion may be successful, but a good Appeal Statement will tie that opinion to the development plan policies.

The Decision Notice that refuses planning permission will list the planning policies of the development plan that the LPA consider relevant. The development plan is the general term for what may be a whole host of differently named plans produced by the LPA, and also possibly by County Councils or regional authorities such as the Greater London Authority. The LPA, and all other authorities, review and update their plans over time, so they will have different dates for adoption. These may have varying titles, such as a Local Plan, or a Core Strategy, or a Development Management Plan, but the Decision Notice will list those most relevant to your proposal.

The development plan policies will all be accessible on the LPA website. It is important to read these. They set out what will, and will not, be granted planning permission. Often the policies are worded rather generally. Policies concerning neighbouring amenity or design, for instance, often contain general aspirations to seek to ensure there is no loss of amenity for existing residents, and that new development is of a high standard of design. But many policies will have specific criteria against which development proposals will be tested. For instance:

- policies relating to extensions may set out numerical thresholds that the LPA do not wish to see breached: dimensions might be given relating to the maximum depth or height of an extension
- certain geographical areas may have policies that set criteria for development, eg the LPA may allow for a particular increase in the floorspace of houses in the Green Belt, or have a policy that sets out a particular density of development in residential areas designated for their spacious character.
- policies relating to the change of use of commercial premises may give thresholds for the number of a certain use, eg they might define a shopping centre and state how many shops they wish to see in that area
- policies may show areas within a town where a certain density of development is sought, or particular uses resisted

The list of potential policies is almost endless. Yet, if the policy is relevant to your proposed development, then the Inspector must determine the appeal against that policy. You therefore need to be aware of it, and address how your development accords with the policy. The LPA will have assessed the proposal against that Policy, and so if you fail to do the same then your case at appeal is at a disadvantage.

There is no need to include the text of all the policies set out on the Decision Notice as this just uses up the word count of 3,000 that the Inspectorate encourages you to meet. You also do not need to include them as an appendix to your Appeal Statement as the LPA must provide the Inspector with a copy of every policy referred to on the Decision Notice.

It is important to realise that you are allowed to include other policies of relevance. The LPA is making the case why permission should be refused. They may not have included reference to policies that are in support of your scheme. For instance, a development for proposed flats in the centre of a town may be refused on the grounds of design, and the LPA is likely to refer to only those policies. But there may be other policies in the development plan that state the LPA is seeking to increase housing, or that housing should be provided in central areas, or where there is good transport link, or that there is a need for small properties. Again, the potential list of relevant policies is endless. You will only know if there are relevant policies that the LPA have not told you about if you read the development plan documents on their website. You should therefore spend time in reading these documents to see if there is help for you.

If there are additional policies that you consider are helpful to your case, which have not been included on the LPA's Decision Notice, then you must provide a copy to the Inspector. They will not be sent by the LPA. You should include them as an Appendix to your Statement. Make sure you include the title page of the relevant development plan which shows the date when the plan was adopted, or published, as the Inspector needs to know the status of any policy.

Example of how the planning policies might be described

Conversion of storage space above a shop to a small flat in a city centre, where permission has been refused on the grounds of inadequate bedroom size and overlooking to a neighbouring house

The Decision Notice refers to Policy H14 (Internal Space Standards) and Policy R8 (Protection of Residential Amenity) of the Anytown Borough Council Development Management Plan 2017 as being relevant to the proposed development. It is agreed these policies are relevant.

There are other policies that are relevant. These are Policy H2 (Spatial Strategy for Housing) of the Anytown Borough Council Core Strategy 2015, and Policy T2 (Increasing the Mix of Uses in Town Centres) of the Anytown Borough Council Development Management Plan 2017. Copies of these policies are attached at Appendix 2.

Supplementary Planning Documents

Decision Notices may also refer to supplementary planning documents. These may appear in a variety of formats, and are produced by LPAs to provide additional information on a wide range of topics. They can be very detailed in their content, setting out strict requirements that LPAs often want to see met in precise detail. There is no obligation, though, for LPAs to produce this sort of document, so it is not always relevant.

These documents are, in procedural terms for the appeal, treated similarly to development plan documents. If the LPA has considered them as relevant then they will be referred to on the Decision Notice, in which case you should read them and have regard to their content and so address them in your submissions. The LPA will also provide a copy of the relevant part of the document to the Inspectorate.

Similarly, if there are supplementary planning documents that help you, then you should refer to them and provide copies of the relevant part with your Appeal Statement. Again, these documents will be available on the LPA website, and it is well worth spending time to investigate if there are any published Documents that assist.

An important difference between supplementary documents and the planning policies, though, is that they do not form part of the development plan. An Inspector therefore is having regard to them as a material consideration. That might be a consideration that reinforces - or outweighs - conclusions made against the planning policies. As mentioned, the documents can often have very detailed criteria, and LPAs can have a tendency to require absolute compliance. But they cannot deal with every possible circumstance that might arise in the planning system, and a key principle of planning is that every application or appeal is determined on its own merits.

Therefore, the content of any supplementary document is only a material consideration and the policies of the development plan have primacy. Hence, if you demonstrate that your proposed development actually accords with the development plan policies, then that is the relevant test for the Inspector in order to allow the appeal.

Example of how supplementary planning documents might be described

A side and rear extension to a house, where permission has been refused on the grounds of the rear extension causing harm to the outlook of the neighbour, and the modern design of the new side extension

The Decision Notice refers to Part 2.3 of the Anytown Borough Council 'Residential Extension Standards' 2012, which sets out dimensions for the depth of extensions, and Part 3.5 of the same document that sets out dimensions for the design of extensions. It is agreed these parts of the document are relevant.

However, also of relevance is Part 1.1 that says the guidelines are not necessarily relevant in every case and so should not be applied rigidly. Also of relevance is Part 2.9 of the Anytown Borough Council 'Design Guide' 2014, which encourages contemporary design in the Borough. Relevant extracts from these documents are attached at Appendix 3.

National planning policies

There are other planning policies that may be of relevance in addition to those of the development plan that are set out by the LPA. A principal consideration may be those produced by the Government, set out in the National Planning Policy Framework (NPPF)
www.gov.uk/guidance/national-planning-policy-framework

The NPPF is the overall strategic policy framework for England and Wales, and so all appeals must be determined in accordance with the NPPF. The NPPF covers matters such as:

- supporting economic development
- seeking high quality design and a good standard of amenity
- promoting urban areas, encouraging the use of brownfield land, protecting the Green Belt and conserving the natural and built environment
- encouraging the conversion of existing buildings and renewable resources
- promoting mixed use developments
- focusing development in sustainable locations
- improving health, social and cultural wellbeing for all

An LPA's development plan should be in conformity with the NPPF, but the NPPF post-dates some plans and so there can be inconsistencies. This means the NPPF might contain policies and support for your development proposals which is not recognised in the development plan.

As a more up-to-date statement of planning policy, the NPPF may take preference over an older development plan. It is therefore worth reading the NPPF to see if there is additional help, and draw that to the Inspector's attention. There is no need to provide extracts from the NPPF, though; Inspectors are familiar with the wording and have their own copies.

The Government has also published Planning Practice Guidance. This supplements the NPPF and wider planning procedure.
www.gov.uk/government/collections/planning-practice-guidance

It covers an extensive range of topics, including design, flooding, natural environment, heritage matters, transport issues. The Guidance often gives advice on the interpretation of policies and processes to be followed. As with the NPPF, this may be useful to your case and can be cited, even if the LPA has not mentioned it. Again, there is no need to provide copies to the Inspector.

Example of how national policy might be described

A new building at a farmstead, to sell produce produced at the farm, which was refused permission the grounds of the location of the farm in a rural area, and the non-traditional design of the building.

The Decision Notice refers to Policy R3 (Development in the Countryside) and Policy D1 (Design of New Development) of the South Barkhamptonshire District Local Plan 2010. These policies pre-date the publication of the NPPF. The NPPF provides support for economic growth in rural areas, through the provision of well-designed new buildings, and promotes the development and diversification of agricultural buildings. The NPPF also requires good design, and attaches great weight to outstanding or innovative designs.

Changes in planning policies

It is very important to realise that the Inspector's decision is made in relation to local and national planning policies at the time of that decision. This means that, if there is a change in development plan policies, supplementary planning documents, or national planning policy between the date of the Decision Notice and the time of lodging the appeal, then you will need to refer to the up-to-date policies in your Statement of Case.

This can be a mistake by appellants, who refer only to the policy at the time of the Decision Notice. A change in local or national policy may be helpful, or hinder the case, so you must get this right.

Example of a change in relevant policies

A new house was refused permission on the ground that it conflicted with the LPA's Supplementary Planning Document setting out car parking standards, and the design of the new house was harmful to the character of a conservation area.

The Decision Notice was dated 4 February 2019 and referred to Policy H8 (Design of New Development) and Policy C2 (Development Within Conservation Areas) of the Northton Borough Local Plan 2012. It is agreed these policies are relevant.

The Decision Notice also referred to Part 4.5 of the Northton Borough Supplementary Planning Document 'Car Parking Standards' 2009, which states that new houses should provide 3 car parking spaces. Since the Decision Notice was issued, the LPA has a new Supplementary Planning Document 'Vehicle Parking Standards for Development in the Borough' 2019. This was adopted on 10 July 2019 and supercedes the previous document. The new requirements for parking are for 2 spaces per dwelling.

Two car parking spaces are proposed for the new house. The change in the Supplementary Planning Document therefore means that there should no longer be any objection on this ground from the LPA. However, it is recognised the issue of the design of the proposed house and the effect on the conservation area remains at dispute with the LPA.

If there is a change in planning policies after the appeal is lodged – and the change is relevant – then you may need to update the Inspector. If the change is a national policy, the Inspectorate themselves may recognise that and contact you asking for comments. But if there is a change in the development plan policy, or any supplementary planning document, then the Inspectorate are less likely to pick that up, so you will need to contact the Inspectorate.

In all but householder and commercial appeals there is the opportunity for further comments once the appeal has been lodged, so you may refer to the update at that time (see the next section of this book for further information on these steps of the appeal process). However, with householder/commercial appeals there is no such stage in proceedings. You would have to ask for special dispensation to make additional, updated submissions. It is within the remit of the Inspectorate to allow those further submissions, and it is case dependent. If they do accept additional submissions then they will give the LPA the opportunity to comment.

PRECEDENT

Other examples of similar developments that have occurred can be relevant to your case, but not always. The trouble with showing a simple list of developments that seem similar is that there may be important differences in the cases from what is proposed.

It may be relevant to provide a generalised list of what appears as similar developments. For instance, if the issue in the appeal is the design of a proposed roof extension and the effect on the character of the area, and if the immediate vicinity sees a number of similar extensions, then that might be part of the character of the area. In this instance a schedule of those may be helpful for the Inspector. Or if the LPA has refused permission for an infill house on the basis of it being too small for the plot, then if there are other houses that have been allowed in recent years on similar plots, they can be brought to the attention of the Inspector.

The problem with providing a list of examples, though, is that the Inspector will not know the background to the grant of permission, unless it is brought to his/her attention. The Inspector can only determine your appeal on the basis of the information submitted, and so will not investigate the background. The LPA is unlikely to provide the background information, and may say there are differences between the cases.

Therefore it may be sensible to provide detailed information to the Inspector on any precedents. This will necessitate some research as to when, and why, planning permission was granted for any case. Clearly, the more recent the precedent the better; if permission was granted when there was a previous development plan then the LPA may say that is of less relevance, since developments must be determined against the current development plan. The LPA's decision on why to grant planning permission will be set out in their Delegated Report or Committee Report, or a precedent may have been granted at appeal by another Inspector. Those documents may therefore be helpful to your case and, if so, it may be sensible to refer to the content in your Appeal Statement and include as an Appendix. The approved drawings may also be relevant to append.

As ever, you do not want to swamp the Inspector with unnecessary information. Very long lists of vaguely relevant cases, or old cases, or copious appendices may be excessive. If detail is to be provided on some examples, then it is important to focus carefully.

GROUNDS OF APPEAL

This is the 'main event' of the Appeal Statement. It is where you explain to the Inspector why your proposed development should be granted planning permission, and where you counter the LPA's reasons for refusal.

Rebutting the LPA's reasons for refusal

In preparing the Statement of Case you should not have regard just to those reasons for refusal set out on the Decision Notice, but you should also read the longer Report on the planning application that will have been produced by the LPA. If the application was refused permission under delegated powers then there will be a Planning Officer's Delegated Report. If the application was refused at a planning committee then there will be a Committee Report. LPAs do not necessarily inform you of these Reports as a matter of course, but they are public documents that you are entitled to see. You may find them easily accessible on the LPA's website, but some LPA's require you to make a written request to view.

Seeing the relevant Report is imperative in preparing your Statement of Case: it will provide a greater explanation of why your planning permission was refused and so enable you to prepare a far more detailed and relevant Statement of Case. It is also important to note that, in the Householder and Commercial appeal processes, the LPA's case is based solely on that Report: they do not have any opportunity to add to their case, nor respond to your Statement. This means that you can prepare a Case in full knowledge of what the other side's objection is, so there should be no surprises in the process.

Similarly, you should read the comments made by third parties during the course of the planning application. This includes any objections by neighbours and submissions by consultees, eg the Highways Authority, the Environment Agency, local pressure groups, etc. They may have made detailed and specific objections to the proposed development which led to the more generalised Reasons for Refusal from the LPA. If you read those detailed comments then you can tailor your Statement of Case to address those specific matters, rather than just provide a generalised submission. As with the Officer's Report, some LPAs make these comments easily available, whilst with other LPAs you may have to write in order to view.

The Decision Notice should have listed those reasons for refusal in a fairly logical order, from which the important issues can be identified. But sometimes the wording can be rather muddled; you can set out the issues that you see are important to address.

Of course, what to include in the Grounds of Appeal entirely depends on that particular case and what to say cannot be provided as a template in this book. It is a well-established principle in planning that every case is determined on its own merits, so you must write your case having regard to everything read so far. In Written Representation appeals there is no further chance to provide any further arguments in support of your case, so you must spend some time on this document. But there are some principles to follow:

- **Focus on differences:** The Statement should respond to the reasons for refusal from the LPA: the area of difference between you and the LPA. But you may still need to have regard to third parties (see later). In appeals against non-determination your Statement will set out why you consider the scheme to be acceptable and you should address the areas in which you anticipate the LPA are most likely to raise objection.
- **Support with evidence:** A well-argued appeal case shows evidence to support the view that planning permission should be granted. This may be with reference to facts, planning policies, precedent, data, etc, but the case will be stronger if there is more than just an assertion.
- **Conciseness**. The Inspector does not want to see lengthy repetition of background information, or discussion of matters irrelevant to the case. But all evidence must of course be provided. If you are referring to documentation to support your case, then you should provide a full reference to that evidence and provide copies or extracts from that evidence, eg data, or analysis of evidence, maps, or copies of case law if cited. Do not include links to websites.
- **Clearly label documents, and check!** The majority of appeal submissions, and the management of cases, is now undertaken online. When documents are received by the Inspectorate the documents may be printed, or they may remain as on-screen documents, so the Inspector may only ever read e-versions. Check before uploading that the

documents read clearly online, that all photographs/documents have reproduced properly so they can be printed and/or read properly on screen. As mentioned previously, label the filenames clearly.

- **Appendices.** If you need to include appendices, make sure they are labelled and cross-referenced into the document. Be sparing with the appendices – you do not want the Inspector to be required to wade through scores of pages in order to find the one relevant reference to which you are trying to draw attention.
- **Additional specialist evidence.** The LPA's refusal may give rise to issues that you consider need to be addressed by specialist evidence produced by appropriate experts. That might, for instance, be on matters such as trees, daylight, ecology. You are entitled to submit this, but the Planning Inspectorate operate the principle that all parties must have a fair chance to review evidence. For Written Representations, Hearings and Inquiries there is a process for any such evidence to be reviewed (see later) but, as noted earlier, Householder and Commercial appeals do not automatically have the process to allow for the LPA or third parties to respond to additional evidence. You should therefore be aware, if you do submit additional specialist evidence, that the Case Officer at the Inspectorate may consider the LPA and third parties should be given the opportunity to comment, in the interests of fairness. In such circumstances the appeal would then be taken out of the Householder/Commercial Appeals Service and transferred over to the Written Representations process.

Other considerations

As mentioned earlier, the LPA's case will be based on the reasons for refusal they set out on their Decision Notice. Those will be the principal issues that need to be addressed. However there may be other considerations that assist your case. These will need to be expanded upon in your Statement. For instance, you may consider there is a need for the type of development you propose, eg housing, or a particular type of business, or there is a need for your business to be in a particular area, then you might be expanding on this kind of point. Or there may be personal circumstances in your favour, eg a need for a particular type of extension to your house to meet the needs.

Planning law says that decisions should be made in accordance with the development plan, unless material considerations indicate otherwise; those considerations are potentially limitless, and so you have a chance to explain this in your Statement.

RESPONSE TO THIRD PARTIES

Do not forget to have regard to what has been said by parties other than the LPA. Remember, the Inspector is considering the case afresh; as if he or she is determining the case in the first instance. This means that the Inspector can refuse permission for the reasons put forward by, say, neighbours, or on the basis of evidence submitted by a consultee at the application stage. The Inspector will receive a copy of any representations made by third parties.

It is likely that most of what concerns third parties has been covered in the LPA's case, and that may well have led to the reasons for refusal, in which case you will have already covered the topic in the main Statement of Case. But if there are additional topics that have been mentioned then these should be addressed and countered. This is commonly forgotten by appellants who think that, if objections from neighbours do not translate to the formal refusal from the LPA, then there is no need to mention the topic. But the Inspector is entitled to agree with those neighbours, so it is sensible to address anything raised by third parties.

CONDITIONS

If the appeal is allowed then planning permission is granted, and this is usually subject to planning conditions. Conditions can be used to regulate the development that has been permitted, eg the hours of operation for a business, or the materials to be used for an extension. Conditions can also be used to require the submission of information that is approved by the LPA prior to commencement of development, eg the LPA may wish to see samples of bricks before an extension is erected and formally approve them first, or specific details about a junction or car parking arrangements might have to be submitted and approved.

The LPA will provide a list to the Inspectorate of their suggested conditions, in the event of the appeal being allowed. There is nothing to stop you doing the same, and this should be included within the Statement of Case. You may wish to volunteer conditions that might overcome certain objections to the development. For instance, you might offer to obscure glaze a certain window to avoid overlooking, or to provide a landscaping scheme to show some sort of screening.

CONCLUSION

An obvious point, but a clear and concise conclusion to the Appeal Statement that summarises your response to the reasons for refusal is advisable.

PLANNING OBLIGATION

The LPA may consider it necessary to enter into a planning obligation in order to secure planning permission. If this is the case then it will have appeared on the Decision Notice and in the Delegated Report or Planning Committee Report.

A planning obligation (it is also sometimes called a legal agreement, s106 agreement or unilateral undertaking) is a mechanism to assist in mitigating the impact of development and typically covers matters such as financial contributions towards certain matters, securing a particular way in which land or buildings are used, ensuring the provision of some form of development, etc. If you do not agree with the LPA that a planning obligation is necessary then you can contest this. The Government's NPPF says that they can only be requested by an LPA where they are necessary to make the development acceptable in planning terms, they are directly related to the development, and they are fairly and reasonably related in scale and kind to the development. If you dispute these points then you will need to explain clearly, with evidence, why you are not providing a planning obligation.

If you accept that you will provide a planning obligation then it must be completed as soon as possible. You should aim to have it signed and executed soon after lodging the appeal in the first few weeks of the appeal timetable, and then sent to the Planning Inspectorate. By the very latest it needs to be submitted before the date of the Inspector's site visit. The Planning Inspector cannot grant permission subject to the completion of a planning obligation – that is a misconception with many appellants – so you must resolve this matter. As a planning obligation concerns legal matters and must be drawn up correctly, you should seek the advice of a solicitor.

KEY POINTS

- Read the Planning Committee report or the planning Officer's Delegated Report, as well as letters from neighbours and consultees made at the time of the planning application, before preparing your Appeal Statement. Your Statement will need to respond to these.
- Try to be concise in the appeal statement - only include descriptions of the application, the scheme, the surrounding area and any precedents as much as is really relevant to the Inspector.
- The LPA will only refer to planning policies they think are relevant. There may be others that help your case.
- If you make reference to other documents or evidence then make sure copies are provided to the Inspector
- Remember to respond to the comments of neighbours and other third parties, even if the LPA did not include their objections as a ground for formally refusing the planning application.
- Set out any conditions that you would accept if permission is granted.
- Do not try to use the Appeal Statement as a way of trying to negotiate or change the refused scheme.

6. What happens next?

In this section you will learn

- What happens after you have lodged the appeal.
- How to check for procedural errors.
- When you must respond to the LPA's case and any further letters from neighbours.
- How to conduct yourself at the Inspector's site visit.

Provided you have sent all the relevant documentation to the Planning Inspectorate, you will receive confirmation from the Inspectorate that the appeal is valid. If you have omitted relevant documents or filled in any parts of the appeal form incorrectly then you will be informed and asked for the correct information. Remember: the deadline for the Inspectorate to receive a correctly completed appeal form – and all the supporting documentations – is 6 months from the date of the Decision Notice (12 weeks for a householder or commercial case). So be careful in checking that what you send is correct, and do not leave the submission to the last moment: if there is an oversight, you may lose your right of appeal. The deadlines are not arbitrary but are set in law, and so they are strictly enforced.

The official 'start date' letter for the appeal will follow sometime after the letter that confirms the appeal is valid. This sets out the timetable for the appeal, which includes the various events that will happen, what further documents you may have to send and when you must send them; you are not given further reminders and, again, deadlines are strictly enforced. The timetable will consist of the following events.

APPEAL QUESTIONNAIRE

Within a week of the start date letter the LPA must send the 'Questionnaire' to the Inspectorate and to the appellant at the same time. This is, literally, a standard questionnaire the Inspectorate requires the LPA to complete that establishes basic information about the case and requires the LPA to send the various documents against which they determined the planning application. It is sensible to check this document and the answers given by the LPA, since they may make errors or exclude relevant information. The questions will cover:

- a requirement to list the relevant planning policies and to provide copies of those policies.
- a list of whether the appeal site is within a designated area, such as conservation area, green belt, in the setting of a listed building, Area of Outstanding Natural Beauty. Check to see this section is completed properly, as mistakes can be made by all parties regarding any particular designations for land.
- whether the LPA agree to the choice of appeal procedure you have requested on your appeal form, ie Written Representations, Hearing, or Inquiry. If they disagree with your choice they must give reasons. If they agree with the Written Representations procedure they must also state if they agree the site can be seen from public land or not. The LPA must also say if they wish the Inspector to view the appeal site from any neighbouring property. You should consider if you agree with the LPA's responses on any of these questions.
- the LPA may provide their list of suggested conditions (they can provide that at the Statement stage – see later). You may wish to comment on the suggested conditions.
- the Planning Officer's Delegated Report or Committee Report on the planning application should be included. You should already have sought this out in order to prepare a strong Statement of Case, but you should check the LPA have provided the full documentation to the Inspectorate.

The Questionnaire will also say if the LPA intend to prepare a further Statement of Case, or just rely on the Delegated/Committee Report.

- third party representations made at the application stage. Again, you should already have seen these, but check to see they are all as already read and reviewed.

If there is a need to respond to the Questionnaire then that can be done at the next stage (see below). However, with a Householder or Commercial Appeal there is no further right to make submissions. Therefore, any response would only be accepted by the Inspectorate if there is a factual error in the LPA's Questionnaire, in which case you should make that clear.

The Questionnaire also confirms that the LPA has, in all appeals except for Householder/Commercial Appeals, informed third parties of the lodging of the appeal. This is because those third parties are allowed to make further submissions at the appeal stage. You can respond to these later, as explained below.

THE LPA'S SUBMISSION OF STATEMENT

Other than in householder and commercial appeals, the LPA must produce their Statement of Case within 5 weeks of the start date letter. This will be sent to you by the Inspectorate. It will expand upon the reasons for refusal and is likely to also respond to your Appeal Statement that you submitted with the lodging of the appeal. However, the LPA is not obliged to prepare a Statement, and they may simply rely on their Planning Officer's Delegated Report, or the Committee Report.

If the case is a non-determination appeal then this Statement will set out the reasons why, if the appeal had not been lodged, the LPA would have refused permission. Essentially, therefore, the Statement serves the same purpose as if the appeal was not running as a non-determination appeal.

Remember that in the householder and commercial appeal processes the LPA do not produce a further Statement. The LPA must rely solely on their formal Decision Notice and the Delegated Report/Committee Report refusing permission.

THIRD PARTY COMMENTS

The 5 week stage is also when you may receive any further comments from third parties (nb not for householder or commercial appeals, as third parties are not permitted to make further submissions in those instances; they reply only on any letters sent to the LPA during the planning application stage).

FINAL COMMENTS

In the Written Representations appeal process, once the LPA's Statement has been received, you have two weeks in which to make any comments in response (other than in householder and commercial appeals, of course, since there is no Statement submitted).

This opportunity for a right of reply to the LPA's Statement can be a very important stage in presenting your case. But it is not to be used merely to repeat what you have already said in the original Appeal Statement: it is to respond to specific points raised by the LPA and to counter their evidence. The Final Comments stage is also not to be used to introduce new evidence or arguments that should have been included in your original Appeal Statement. The Inspectorate are strict on this, and any new evidence that does not strictly respond to the LPA's Statement will be returned.

The Final Comments stage is also when you may respond to any additional representations made by third parties. Similarly, any response must not raise new points, but can only refer to points raised by those third parties.

A common matter to include in the Final Comments stage is a response to any conditions suggested by the LPA. Their Statement will typically include a list of planning conditions that, if the Inspector is minded to allow the appeal, the LPA wishes to see attached to the grant of planning permission. The Inspector is not obliged to simply accept these without question. He/she will consider each one in turn to see if it meets the Government's tests for attaching planning conditions; namely that they are necessary, relevant to planning, relevant to the development to be permitted, enforceable, precise, and reasonable. If you believe that a particular condition does not meet these tests then explain in your Final Comments why that is the case.

If you agree with the LPA's suggested conditions then there is no need to specifically comment. However, it is worth commenting on any 'pre-commencement' conditions that are suggested. These are conditions that are phrased with wording such as *'no development shall take place until...'* or *'prior to any works starting on site...'* Whilst these are allowed to be attached, the Government discourages their use and so the law now requires there to be written agreement from the appellant for a pre-commencement condition. This means that if the LPA is proposing a condition worded this way – and you are content with that condition – then you should say in your Final Comments that you agree to it.

You can also suggest your own conditions if you think they may address a concern of the LPA or third parties. For instance, if a neighbour or the LPA is objecting to potential overlooking from a window then, if not already suggested, you could propose a planning condition that requires a certain window to be obscure glazed, or to be fixed shut.

Similar principles apply to the preparation of Final Comments as with the preparation of the Appeal Statement, namely:

- Focus on what specific differences remain. If the LPA have countered your case, and you consider you have something to add to counter back, then focus on the relevant point. Do not just repeat what you have said in your initial Appeal Statement for the sake of it.

- Remain concise. The Final Comments response should be short and targeted even more on just the points that are important. This stage is therefore helpful for putting a punchy final submission to the Inspector.
- Provide evidence if needed. Although the Final Comments stage is limited in the scope for submissions, if the LPA or third parties have raised something that necessitates a response or clarification on a technical matter then you can make such a submission of reply.

There is no Final Comments stage at a Hearing or Inquiry, as the expectation is that any response is made verbally as part of the discussions that arise during those events.

As noted earlier, your development might lead to a need for a legal agreement. If a signed and executed agreement has not yet been submitted with the lodging of the appeal or with any response to the Questionnaire, then the Final Comments stage should be the objective; any later, and the Inspector may not see it before the site visit.

INSPECTOR'S SITE VISIT

In Written Representation appeals the Inspectorate will arrange a date and time for the Inspector to view the property. This will be in accordance with the submissions by the appellant and the LPA regarding whether the visit needs to enter private land. If that is the case then an 'access required' site visit is arranged: you will be informed of a time period when the Inspector will come to the site, and you are required to provide access during that time.

The site visit itself is usually a fairly formal affair, and led by the Inspector. He or she will know what they want to see on the site. With Written Representation cases, the site visit is not the opportunity to discuss the merits of the case with the Inspector: the decision is based on the written submissions, and the site visit is there for the Inspector to see the physical features of the site and surroundings.

Although the Inspector knows what to look for, and the event is quite formalised, you should ensure that the Inspector does not depart without seeing everything you wish to be seen. You are allowed to check the Inspector has viewed everything you have referred to in your submissions: both on the site and in the wider area, if you have already mentioned that.

An Inspector may have been asked to view the appeal site from neighbouring land or properties. That will be carried out under the same procedure of the Inspector only viewing physical features and not entering into any discussions of the case.

DOS

- Do make sure you are at the site before the stated time. You then have time to check the site is accessible, locks and gates open, paths are clear, etc. And the Inspector may, of course, turn up slightly early.
- Do refresh yourself with the scheme drawings and all documentation, so you are ready to answer any questions if the Inspector asks.
- Do be confident to ask if the Inspector has all the right drawings and documents.
- Do be aware of how the Inspector wants to run the site visit - it varies. Some like to walk around by themselves, others may wish to have matters explained to them. So don't impose on the Inspector if they want to be alone.
- Do point out any physical features on the site that you want the Inspector to see, but don't make any subjective comment on issues. For instance, you could say 'That is the tree and the neighbour's window referred to in the reason for refusal', but you could not say 'You can see that tree is far enough from the neighbour's window to mean there isn't any overshadowing'.
- Do ensure you are happy the Inspector has seen everything on the site before he/she leaves.

DON'TS

- Don't complain and grumble about how the LPA have refused permission, or about your neighbours, or that you were unfairly treated! The Inspector has arrived to look at the site and judge the current appeal.
- Don't be offended if the Inspector refuses even simple hospitality
- Don't object if the Inspector says he/she is viewing from your neighbour. All parties' opinions must be considered, and that viewing will be carried out the same impartial way.
- Don't try to give any extra evidence at the site visit, such as documents or photographs. It will be rejected.

If the appeal site can be seen from public land then an 'unaccompanied' site visit is arranged. In that case you will not be informed, as the Inspector does not need to enter land.

A site visit is held as part of the Hearing or Inquiry process. Discussion might occur at the site visits as part of those events (see below).

HEARINGS

If the appeal is following the Hearing route then you will be informed of the date and venue around 10 weeks after the start of the appeal. The Planning Inspectorate are likely to have canvassed your opinion on possible dates prior to confirming this.

A Hearing is an informal discussion, led by the Inspector. He/she will have produced an agenda that list the topics to be discussed. These are most likely to be based on the reasons for refusal set out on the LPA's decision notice and the evidence set out in your Statement of Case. The preparation for a Hearing is therefore very similar to a Written Representations appeal, in that you must produce a comprehensive and well-argued Appeal Statement (see previous Chapter).

Prior to the Hearing you will also have been expected to produce a Statement of Common Ground with the LPA. This sets out the matters that are not in dispute, with the objective of clarifying and speeding up the discussion at the Hearing. The Statement of Common Ground is usually initiated by the appellant, and is a very helpful document to focus discussions and ensure the Hearing is run as efficiently as possible; Inspectors like good Statements if they contain substantive agreements. You should therefore try to agree as much as possible as early as possible with the LPA.

You are able to add any other topics to the Inspector's agenda at the Hearing. You want to ensure that everything relevant to your case is discussed. Hearings can be attended by third parties, and they similarly may add topics for discussion. However, the Hearing is not an opportunity to submit additional evidence that should have been included within your Appeal Statement; the Inspector will be strict about any attempt to slip through the strict deadlines on submission of evidence by appellants attempting to bring along additional evidence not seen by the LPA, unless there are very good reasons.

After the Inspector introduces a topic for discussion, he/she will ask the appellant for their view on that topic. The LPA will reply verbally with their opinion. Third parties might comment. The appellant then has the verbal right of reply. The Inspector may follow this process with direct questions to any party.

The process can be slightly stilted and perhaps less informal than the Hearing system was intended to be, due to the convention of statements and rights of reply being followed. If you consider your point has not been covered then this means you need to be bold in speaking up: it can be the case that the discussion moves on to a new topic with you realising that not everything has been covered, or that a full response to the LPA or third parties has not been given. You do not want to leave a Hearing thinking there were gaps in the discussion.

The key to a Hearing is preparation. You will have produced your own Appeal Statement with the lodging of the appeal, you will have received the LPA's Statement at the 5 week stage, and you will have received all the submissions from third parties. You should therefore read all that documentation carefully in order to be ready to make your case, and so any verbal submission from others is less likely to be a surprise. Make notes on your case to ensure on the day you are ready to cover everything that you want to say, and you know what the LPA are likely to say.

Hearings will contain a discussion on possible conditions that can be attached to a grant of permission. The same principles as said earlier with relation to the Questionnaire follow, ie that you can suggest your own conditions and can critique the LPA's.

The Hearing will usually reconvene on the same day as a site visit. This is accompanied by both the appellant and a representative from the LPA, and discussions may continue on the site. Third parties may ask to be present at the site visit; if it is private land you are not obliged to allow access, but you may see no harm in their attendance.

INQUIRIES

If the appeal is following the Inquiry route then the date of the Inquiry takes on a particular significance. As with the Hearing, the Inspectorate will inform you of the date. This will have been in consultation with the appellant and the LPA, since there is likely to be legal representation and so a number of different people to coordinate. If your appeal is progressing through an Inquiry then your legal advisor should be giving you full advice on the preparation of the case and the coordination necessary for the process.

Once the Inquiry date is set then the Inspectorate will inform you of the date for the submission of 'Proofs of Evidence', which is 4 weeks before the date of the Inquiry. A Proof of Evidence is essentially a detailed Statement of Case, and so is likely to expand in even greater detail the matter first raised in the Appeal Statement (discussed in the previous Chapter). The Proofs may cover a number of topics, eg town planning matters, trees, highways, noise.

The LPA will also be producing their Proofs of Evidence, and a Statement of Common Ground is also produced. As with a Hearing, the Inspectorate exchange these between the parties and the right of reply exists at the Inquiry stage. And, as with a Hearing, the submission of late evidence at the Inquiry in an attempt to get around the strict deadlines is frowned upon by the Inspector.

The process at an Inquiry is very formalised. There is likely to be formal opening statements by legal representatives, and then evidence is presented verbally with formal cross-examination by advocates. The Inspector will also take an inquisitorial role and thoroughly question you. Third parties may also appear at the Inquiry to present evidence

As with a Hearing, there is a site visit at an Inquiry, where there may be continued discussions regarding the case.

THE INSPECTOR'S DECISION

After the site visit, regardless of the process, in due course the outcome everyone has waited for arrives: the Inspector's decision on the appeal. This will either allow the appeal or dismiss it, and is written in the form of a letter that explains in detail the reasons the appeal is allowed or dismissed.

LEGAL CHALLENGES

There is no right of further appeal against the Inspector's decision merely because you disagree with the decision. There is only a right for a High Court challenge against a decision if it can be proven the Inspector made an error in law, eg misinterpreting or misapplying a policy, or failing to take account of an important consideration, and the High Court must be persuaded that such an event might have affected the outcome of the decision. A challenge must be made within 42 days of the date of the decision.

If the High Court decides there was an error in law then the appeal is returned to the Planning Inspectorate for re-determination. This does not necessarily mean a different decision is reached, as the appeal is simply looked at afresh.

Due to the complex legal issues in this course of action, and the likely high costs, legal advice should always be sought if a High Court challenge is considered as this book cannot cover all possible matters.

MINOR ERRORS IN THE DECISION

Occasionally an Inspector may make a minor error in the decision, eg a drafting error that cites the wrong application number, an incorrect reference to approved plans, the wrong address etc. These may not materially affect the decision, but you might consider they cause some issues for you in the future, eg if the drawing numbers are listed incorrectly then there could be confusion at a later date as to what is the approved scheme.

In the past these errors, although minor, could also only have been corrected through the High Court. But fortunately now the Inspectorate is allowed to correct these through what is known as the 'Slip Rule'. If there is a simple error that can be corrected then you should write to the Inspectorate requesting a change, and this must be done within 42 days of the decision letter.

KEY POINTS

- Once the appeal is running you will receive procedural documents from the Inspectorate. Check these are correct and complete, and do not be afraid of querying anything you think may be wrong, or don't understand
- Keep to the timetable for any submissions to the Inspectorate. They will not be changed and you will not get reminders.
- Use the Final Comments stage to make an effective response to the LPA's Statement and any third party comments. It is your chance to enhance your case
- Prepare for the Inspector's site visit, and ensure you are content he/she has seen everything before leaving
- If you are proceeding with a Hearing or Inquiry, prepare very thoroughly before the event!
- Respond to suggested conditions at the Final Comments stage. You can question the conditions and suggest your own, but also agree with any pre-commencement conditions if you are content with them

7. Costs

In this section you will learn

- When you can apply for costs.
- How to apply for costs.
- How to avoid costs being awarded against you.

The appeal process contains the opportunity to apply for costs to be awarded. However, unlike the Courts system, costs do not automatically follow the decision, ie you will not simply be awarded costs from the LPA if you win the appeal. The objective of the costs regime is to encourage reasonable behaviour by all parties, to ensure a timely and efficient appeal process. This means that costs are only awarded if there has been unreasonable behaviour by the LPA, and if that behaviour has led to an unnecessary appeal or wasted time.

Before making an application for an award for costs you should, therefore, carefully consider if the LPA have behaved unreasonably. You may not agree with their decision to refuse planning permission, but if it is a matter of judgement on the merits of a case then you will need to ask yourself if that really was an unreasonable refusal, or really just down to a difference of opinion.

If successful, the costs that can be claimed are limited to those accrued through the appeal process, which is commonly the time spent on any fees for the production of evidence in support of your case. Costs expended during the course of the planning application are not reimbursed, nor is there any compensation for the delay caused by the appeal process.

THE BASIS FOR A COSTS AWARD

Costs can be awarded on two basis: a **procedural award** or a **substantive award**.

Procedural award

A procedural costs award relates to the appeal process. LPAs are expected to behave reasonably in relation to how an appeal runs, and if they fail in that requirement, costs might be awarded. The Government has examples of what might constitute unreasonable behaviour by an LPA on procedural matters:

- lack of co-operation with you during the appeal, or delay in providing information or keeping to deadlines.
- only supplying relevant information at appeal when you had previously requested it at the application stage.
- not agreeing a statement of common ground, or factual matters, in a timely manner.
- introducing fresh and substantial evidence at a late stage in the appeal process that leads to an adjournment.
- prolonging an appeal by introducing a new reason for refusal, or withdrawing a reason for refusal.
- failing to attend a site visit if required, or a Hearing or Inquiry, without good reason, or failure to notify the public of a Hearing or Inquiry where this leads to an adjournment.
- providing information that is shown to be manifestly inaccurate or untrue, or the deliberate concealment of relevant evidence.
- In an appeal against non-determination the LPA should explain their reasons for not reaching a decision within the time limit, and why permission would not have been granted in any event. If the appeal is

allowed then costs may be awarded as there were no reasons to justify delaying the determination.

This is not an exhaustive list – there may be other procedural matters that lead to unreasonable behaviour.

Substantive award

A substantive award relates to the LPA's behaviour with regards to the matters under consideration at the appeal itself, eg by unreasonably refusing permission or unreasonably defending appeals. This is the most common basis for making costs application, and the Government has examples of what might constitute unreasonable behaviour:

- failure to produce evidence to substantiate each reason for refusal on appeal.
- vague, generalised or inaccurate assertions about a proposal's impact, which are unsupported by any objective analysis.
- preventing or delaying development which should clearly be permitted, having regard to planning policies and material considerations.
- refusing planning permission on a planning ground capable of being dealt with by conditions where suitable conditions would enable the proposed development to go ahead.
- acting contrary to well-established case law.
- persisting in objections to a scheme or elements of a scheme where an Inspector in a previous appeal has previously indicated to be acceptable.
- not determining similar cases in a consistent manner.
- failing to grant a further planning permission for a scheme that is the subject of an extant or recently expired permission where there has been no material change in circumstances.

- refusing to approve reserved matters when the objections relate to issues that should already have been considered at the outline stage.
- imposing a condition that is not necessary or relevant.
- requiring that the appellant enters into a planning obligation which does not accord with the law or relevant national policy.
- refusing to enter into pre-application discussions, or to provide reasonably requested information, when a more helpful approach would probably have resulted in either the appeal being avoided altogether or the issues to be narrowed.
- not reviewing their case promptly following the lodging of an appeal against refusal of planning permission (or non-determination).

The first three examples are the most common reasons that appellants seek costs against the LPA: the appellant thinks that the LPA have been vague about the reason for refusal, and have not supported their case well enough. If you are thinking of making an application for an award of costs, be objective if you think these are your grounds. Has the LPA really been vague and not provided proper evidence? Or is it actually just a difference of opinion on, say, what the effects of an extension are on a neighbour's privacy, or whether a tree can withstand pruning, or if deliveries at a certain time of day are too noisy? Inspectors are loathe to stray into areas where there is a simple disagreement in matters of judgement. Try to be rational and think whether – even though you disagree with the final decision to refuse permission – there is some merit in the LPA's case.

Again, this list is not exhaustive; there may be other reasons for seeking a substantive award of costs.

FULL OR PARTIAL COSTS

An award of costs can be made in full, meaning all the costs you have accrued in preparing the appeal and evidence, and submitting the appeal and any costs application, can be claimed.

A partial award of costs is where there has been unreasonable behaviour that does not relate to all areas of the appeal. For instance, if a planning application for a new house had been refused on the grounds of alleged poor access and effect on the light of a neighbouring property, you had commissioned an expert to provide highways evidence and an expert on lighting, then late in the appeal process the LPA were found to have acted unreasonably by having made an error on the highways refusal, only partial costs would be awarded with regards to the highways evidence.

COSTS AGAINST YOU

It should be remembered that the LPA can seek an award of costs against the appellant. Again, this can be on the basis of a procedural award or a substantive award if you behave unreasonably. The Government's guidance on when this might occur is broadly similar to that relating to LPAs, and includes the following circumstances:

- the development is clearly not in accordance with the development plan and no other material considerations are advanced that indicate the decision should have been made otherwise, or there is inadequate supporting evidence.
- the appeal follows a recent appeal decision in respect of the same, or a very similar, development on the same, or substantially the same site where an Inspector decided that the proposal was unacceptable and circumstances have not materially changed in the intervening period.

- lack of co-operation with the LPA, or other parties, in providing information, or discussing the application or appeal, or a failure to adhere to deadlines.
- only supplying relevant information at appeal when it was requested, but not provided, at application stage.
- introducing fresh and substantial evidence at a late stage in the appeal necessitating an adjournment, or extra expense for preparatory work.
- prolonging the proceedings by introducing a new ground of appeal or issue
- not completing a timely statement of common ground or not agreeing factual matters.
- providing information that is shown to be manifestly inaccurate or untrue, or deliberately concealing evidence at the application stage or appeal.
- failing to attend or to be represented at a site visit, Hearing or Inquiry without good reason.
- withdrawal of an appeal without good reason.

The first two examples can be particularly relevant to costs' awards against appellants. In short, if you are pursuing an appeal that is so clearly against planning policies then you are at risk of losing that appeal with costs against you. Similarly, if you are pursuing an appeal that is very similar to a previously dismissed appeal then you are at risk. For these reasons you need to go back to the first principles set out in this book: think before you make an appeal whether there is a compromise or change you can make to the LPA, and do not just rush into an appeal on the simple basis that you are convinced you are right.

The last example is also important to remember. If there is good reason to withdraw an appeal then you should do so as soon as possible. If an appeal is withdrawn without any material change in circumstances relevant to the planning issues arising on the appeal, an award of costs may be made against you if another party has incurred wasted expense.

APPLYING FOR COSTS

Seeking an award for costs is termed making an application for an award of costs, and must be made in accordance with certain time limits. Late costs applications are very rarely accepted. In Written Representations and in Householder/Commercial Appeals, if you consider that there are reasonable grounds for making an application for costs at the lodging of the appeal, then you should make the submission at this time.

With Written Representation appeals it may not be until the receipt of the LPA's Statement at the 5 week stage that you consider there are grounds for making an award of costs, in which case you will need to submit the claim by the Final Comments stage. At Hearings or Inquiries a costs application can be made at any time, including at the Hearing/Inquiry itself.

If the costs application relates to mattes at the Inspector's site visit then that needs to be made within 7 days of the site visit.

In all instances, the LPA have a right of reply to the application for an award of costs. The appellant then has a further right of reply. The Inspector will make the final decision, which is in a separate letter to the main planning appeal, which will allow the claim (in full or partially) or refuse the claim.

KEY POINTS

- Costs can only be awarded if there is 'unreasonable behaviour' - they do not follow the outcome of the appeal decision.
- You can only claim for costs that arise during the appeal process, not any before then or any compensation for delay.
- There are strict deadlines for lodging an application for award of costs.
- Think objectively before applying for costs - have the LPA really behaved unreasonably, or is it actually just a difference of views?
- You are at risk of costs being awarded against you if you behave unreasonably.

8. Appeals against conditions

In this section you will learn

- Why planning conditions are attached, and the tests they must meet.
- How you can appeal against a condition you dispute.
- Potential dangers in this type of appeal, and how to avoid risk.

Planning permission granted by the LPA is most likely to be subject to a number of planning conditions. If you do not agree with those then there is a right of appeal.

The Government's guidance on the use of planning conditions is that they should only be attached if they meet **all** of the following tests:

1. necessary;
2. relevant to planning;
3. relevant to the development to be permitted;
4. enforceable;
5. precise; and
6. reasonable in all other respects

If you feel a planning condition attached to a grant of planning permission does not satisfy all these tests – **all six must be met** – then you can appeal to have the condition either removed or modified.

Examples

1 Planning permission may have been granted for the change of use of a café with hours of use until 6pm as the LPA considers any later use would be harmful to neighbouring amenity. You may see that as unreasonable, as you believe a later use to 8pm would still be acceptable. You can appeal to seek variation of that condition to the later opening hours as you think it is not necessary or reasonable.

2 You may have been granted permission for an extension to a house but the LPA requires you to stop using one of your two driveway access points, as they consider there to be harm to the highway otherwise. You may see that as not necessary or relevant, as you may be of the view both access points remain safe. You can appeal to seek removal of that condition.

An appeal can be made directly against a condition attached to a grant of planning permission. The normal 6 month deadline for this applies and the appeal should be made in the same manner as explained before. You will need to prepare the Appeal Statement as before, but in this instance you need to particularly concentrate on why the condition does not meet all of the six tests set out above. Your Appeal Statement should also clearly set out what you want changed: either how the condition should be modified, or why you want it deleted completely.

The appeal runs through the normal timetable of events after lodging, ie the LPA will make their case, you can respond, and there will be an Inspector's site visit.

It is very important to realise, though, that in making an appeal directly against a condition attached to a grant of planning permission that the Planning Inspector has the power to reverse or vary any part of the planning permission already granted by the LPA. This means the original permission is at risk: the Inspector considers the development as if it was an application made to him/her in the first instance, and so is able to refuse permission for that original grant of permission even if the LPA granted permission, or change that permission by altering other conditions.

This power of the Inspector is only occasionally used, but it is a risk. You may lose your original planning permission, or it may be varied in some way. Before lodging an appeal against a condition you should, therefore, think back to the first principles in this book: is an appeal necessary, and can I compromise with the LPA? If a compromise can be made then you can make an application to remove or modify a condition attached to a planning permission (sometimes called a s73 application).

You also have a right of appeal against a refusal of a s73 application that seeks planning permission to carry out development without complying with a condition which has been imposed on a planning permission. This runs in the same manner as other appeals, ie with the 6 month deadline from any refusal of the application (or non-determination), the need for submitting an Appeal Statement, and the usual timetable for submission of evidence.

The significant difference between an appeal against refusal of a s73 application and an appeal directly against a grant of planning permission is that the original permission is not at risk with a s73 appeal. The Planning Inspector can only look at the condition in dispute. He/she is able to modify or remove other conditions attached to the original grant of planning permission, but cannot reverse that original grant of permission. For this reason, you may consider it safer to pursue any dispute in conditions through the s73 route first, and then appeal if necessary.

KEY POINTS

- Planning conditions must satisfy all six tests of the Government's guidance.
- If you are not happy with a planning condition attached to a grant of planning permission you have a right of appeal.
- An appeal against conditions attached to a grant of permission runs the risk of losing the original permission, although this is a small risk.
- You can make an application to the LPA to remove or vary a planning condition, and there is a right of appeal against any refusal or non-determination.

7. Ready to appeal?

Everyone who submits a planning application would like it to be approved. But there are always differences of opinion in how land should be developed and how buildings should be used. The planning system is there to weigh up the arguments from all sides, and it has to be accepted that sometimes the planning application that you think is so clearly acceptable is judged differently by others.

The appeal process is there to give a fair and impartial review of the decision-making process. But it is a lengthy and complex process, and is usually a last resort: a favourable decision is what you are after, but an adverse decision might blight the land for some time. So it is very important to think carefully before appealing, and first consider if there is an alternative. Can you amend the scheme in some simple way to overcome the concerns of the LPA or your neighbours? Can you discuss the various options with the Planning Officer? Was there, if you are honest, something lacking in your original planning application that made the LPA come to the decision they did, eg you could have provided more information about the effect on trees, or light, or ecology? If so, then it may be better to try to resolve the situation with a new application to the Council; usually there is a 'free go' with a resubmission where you do not have to pay any further planning application fee. The process may be quicker and more certain.

But sometimes there will be little compromise possible. The LPA's demands may make the scheme unworkable, unviable or simply not attractive to build. A golden rule in planning is to only get planning permission for something you actually want to build; anyone can get permission for something, but remember that permission may be the only permission you obtain. There is no point in compromising with the LPA to get a planning permission you never intend to build if, for example, it does not provide you with the additional space you need. That is a waste of time and money.

In that case an appeal is worthwhile. The appeals system is truly independent, and you will have a fair review of the case. But as it is a process that requires a judgement to be made on the basis of submitted evidence, it is clearly important to put your case as well as possible. The advice in this book will have helped you make your case, and so good luck.

8. Using professionals

This book has set out how to prepare and submit your own planning appeal, respond to the LPA's statement of case and third party submissions, and how to liaise with the Planning Inspectorate. You may need the help of professionals in the appeal to make the best case. This is particularly the case if there are technical issues raised in the reasons for refusal, such as:

- **Arboriculturists** to address tree issues
- **Drainage consultants** for matters such as sustainable drainage, flooding
- **Highways consultants** who can advise on safe access, parking provision, traffic generation
- **Surveyors** who can provide evidence on structural issues, day and sunlight, access and boundary matters
- **Noise consultants** if issues relate to impact of a scheme on existing neighbours or future occupiers of a building
- **Air quality consultants** where the quality of the surrounding environment or internal space is a concern
- **Ecologists** whose expertise is likely if there is any issue relating to protected species

- **Energy consultants** since LPAs are increasingly aware of the need to minimise the use of energy
- **Solicitors** will be necessary for legal agreements, and advice on matters relating to legal precedent

You can, of course, pass the appeal over to a professional agent to handle from beginning to end, and such a role is commonly undertaken by **town planning consultants** or **architects**.

Appendix 1: Appeals in Sussex and Kent

APPEALS CASEWORK PORTAL FOR EAST SUSSEX, WEST SUSSEX AND KENT

Chapter 4 of this book outlined the submission process for appeals throughout most of the country and so most appellants will be following the guidance in Chapter 4.

But if your LPA is within these three counties then you will be directed on the Portal to a different system which is currently (as of 2020) in trial mode. The trial system is similar to many other Government form-filling websites, such as tax returns, driving licences, passports, etc as it leads you through various questions and is more intuitive in showing what information needs to be provided.

STARTING WITH THE TRIAL PORTAL SYSTEM

The Portal explains that you are asked some pre-qualifying questions to determine if you can use the new system for your appeal. If not, you will be directed back to the original Appeals Casework Portal, in which case return to Chapter 4 of this book for advice.

If your case meets the new requirements then you will be shown a screen confirming this (the wording may vary, depending on the type of application that was refused permission by the LPA):

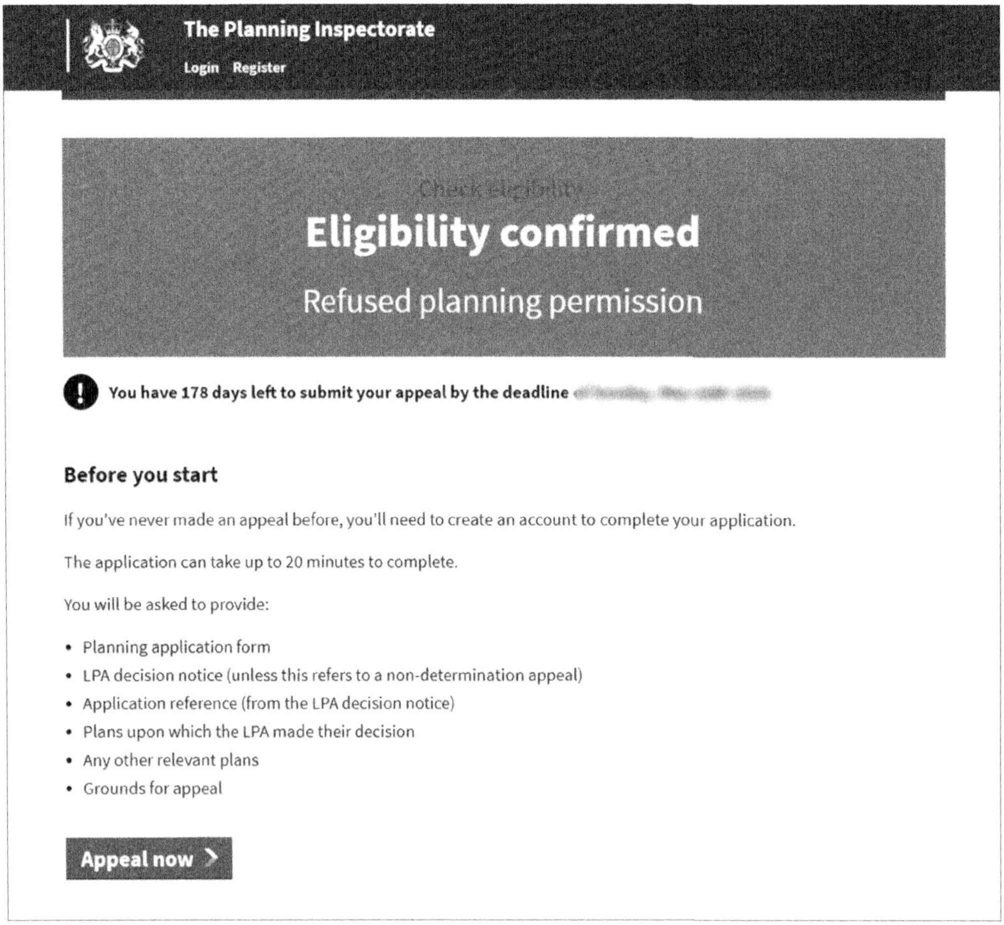

The screen also confirms how long you have to lodge your appeal, which relates to the statutory deadline for appeals, and reminds you what documentation you are going to be needing to make the appeal. You will need to create an online account to be able to lodge the appeal, and this is done after you click the 'Appeal now' button.

Once you have registered, you will be presented with your homepage that lists your current appeals. Messages from the Portal will also appear here. If this is your first case there will not be any appeals listed. To lodge a new appeal click on 'Appeals' on the menu bar.

You will be taken through a further link to start a new appeal, and this will then bring up the key screen for the new appeal that sets out progress:

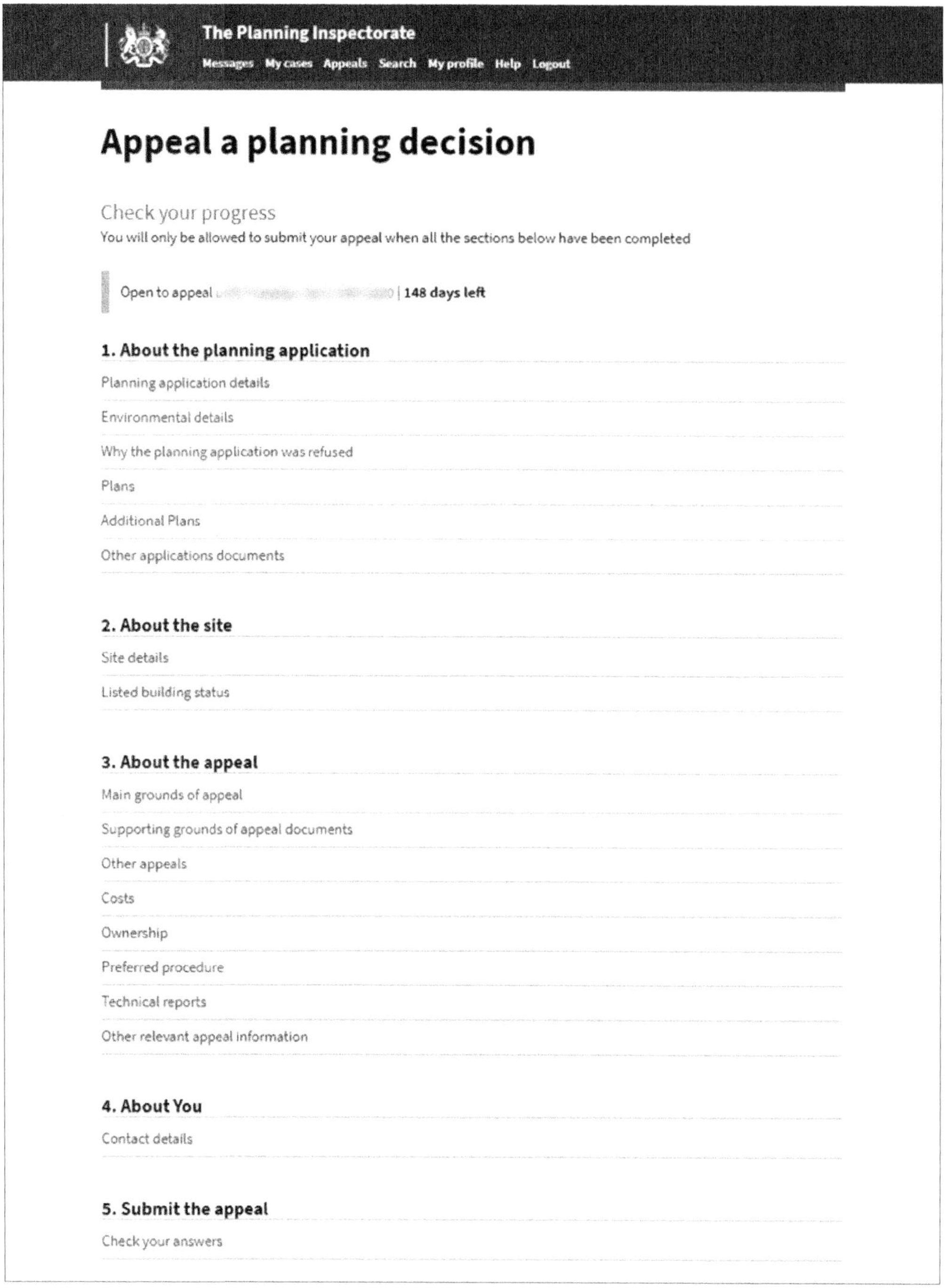
The Planning Inspectorate

Messages My cases Appeals Search My profile Help Logout

Appeal a planning decision

Check your progress

You will only be allowed to submit your appeal when all the sections below have been completed

Open to appeal | **148 days left**

1. About the planning application

Planning application details

Environmental details

Why the planning application was refused

Plans

Additional Plans

Other applications documents

2. About the site

Site details

Listed building status

3. About the appeal

Main grounds of appeal

Supporting grounds of appeal documents

Other appeals

Costs

Ownership

Preferred procedure

Technical reports

Other relevant appeal information

4. About You

Contact details

5. Submit the appeal

Check your answers

This long screen sets out all the information that is required to be filled out in order to lodge the appeal. It is the same information on the existing main Portal, but has been sub-divided more than the main system. This new trial system also allows you to enter parts of the form and return to the submission more easily than the main system.

COMPLETING THE PORTAL'S FORMS

You will find that once you enter into one section of the form, eg the 'Planning application details' section, or the 'Why the planning application was refused' section, that this is followed by many more click-through links asking single questions that is seen on the main Portal. This means there are potentially scores of questions to answer. As the system is more intuitive in leading you through the questions and setting out what documents need to be uploaded at various points, then it is generally more straightforward. The following sets out advice on these sections of the online form. However, with so many questions this book is not going to replicate every screenshot, as it would be far too long and many parts would be irrelevant to many readers.

The following section of this book, therefore, outlines the individual sections of the overall appeal form. Certain sections of the form require you to upload documentation. As you will have seen from the main page of the Portal, your appeal must be lodged with the Inspectorate by a certain deadline. This deadline includes the Inspectorate receiving all correct supporting documentation. It is therefore extremely important that you check and double check what you are sending before uploading. The online appeal submission will only be checking a document is uploaded, not that it is the correct document. That is done at a later date by a Case Officer at the Planning Inspectorate. If that Officer finds you have omitted the correct document, or it is incomplete, then you may miss the deadline. Bear in mind that the check by the Inspectorate on validation may be some days or weeks after you submit the appeal, so if that validation check then falls beyond the 12 week/6 month deadline, you could be out of time. You will have missed your chance to appeal.

It is advisable to upload your documents as pdfs, to ensure no errors when they are received by the Inspectorate. Label the filenames sensibly: you want to make life easy for the Case Officer at the Inspectorate, so that your documents reach the Inspector correctly and as clear as possible. So filenames should have the name of the document (eg 'Decision Notice 5 Jan 2020', or 'Design and Access Statement Oct 2019'), if there are more than one part to a document then label logically (eg 'Appeal Statement Appendix 1 Photographs', or 'Tree survey part 1 of 3'). If you are uploading drawings then label them with the drawing number and paper size too (eg 'Rear elevation 05A at A3 size', or 'site plan 01 at A4 size').

Planning application details

The questions in this section lead you through the application that was refused by the LPA. You are first asked to confirm the name of the appellant. The appellant must be the same as the applicant who was named on the planning application form submitted to the LPA (though if there is more than one applicant, the appellant can be all of them, or just one). Therefore ensure this question is answered correctly: the right of appeal only lies with the applicant, and if the wrong person tries to claim the right for the appeal it may be invalid.

The name of the LPA and the reference number for the planning application is then asked for. You will find this on the Decision Notice or validation letter you received from the LPA. The type of planning application is also asked for, with a series of tick-boxes. If your application was for certain types of development then that might lead to a further series of questions. For instance, residential development leads to a question as to whether you will raise an issue of '5 year housing land supply' in your Appeal Statement, and whether the development relates to a House in Multiple Occupation. Some commercial developments require you to measure the site. There is a drop-down menu on the page to help you with how to answer these questions.

You are asked to 'Provide the description of development, as detailed in the original planning application form', which is a simple question of just filling in what you wrote on your application form. The question following this is 'Has the description of the development changed?' It is a common misconception that the LPA can alter the description of a proposed development. However, in fact, this can only be done if the applicant has agreed to such a change. This is an important matter: you want to be granted planning permission for what you want to build, ie the plans you have submitted, together with the description of the development, comprise that permission.

Therefore, if the LPA has changed the description of the development by the time they issue their Decision Notice, you are not obliged to agree with that description. If you described it in a particular way on the planning application form and you are not content with the LPA's description on their validation letter or their Decision Notice, then you should click 'No'. The Inspector should use your description. Having said that, an LPA is able to clarify, or 'tidy up', a description. For instance, if the application form has put an excessively lengthy description of works that are irrelevant, or mistaken, then the LPA may have reworded parts, and an Inspector is likely to do the same.

If you had agreed with the LPA a modified description of the proposal during the course of the planning application you would click 'Yes' in response to the question 'Has the description of the development changed?'. This may have been either at validation or perhaps if amendments were made to the proposed development before it was refused permission. In that case the question asks you to explain why the description has changed.

The form then continues with you required to upload the application form. Make sure all pages are submitted. This needs to include the pages that show the ownership certificate that is dated and signed, and the last page of the application form that is dated and signed. Note that if you download a copy of the application form off the LPA's website, some LPAs remove the signature for data protection purposes. The Inspectorate need the full signed and dated copy, so ensure you send them that. Again, a partial form is not a valid form.

This section of the form finally requires you to upload the LPA's Decision Notice. Again, ensure this is a full copy with all pages: LPAs differ in how they produce these, and some Notices have all the information on one page, whilst others may have a title page and a schedule of reasons for refusal on a second page. A partial Decision Notice is not a complete Notice, and if you fail to send the whole document within the deadline then you may have an invalid appeal.

Environmental details

This section is a short series of questions that is relevant if an Environmental Impact Assessment accompanied the planning application.

Plans

This section is a simple requirement to upload the plans upon which the decision by the LPA was made. The main Portal has a far more complicated requirement for uploading plans, and so it may be tempting to just fill in this section simply. However, the issue of plans is often complicated in appeals. The plans submitted with the application might have been amended after it was lodged, or additional information submitted to address comments by the LPA. Not all LPAs list the refused plan numbers on their Decision Notice, and errors can be made.

Clarifying drawing and documents is a matter that is commonly overlooked by appellants. You want to make sure the Inspector grants permission for the scheme you intend to build: the Inspector's decision will list the approved drawing numbers, so it is to your advantage to make this procedural matter clear. Therefore, although not a requirement of the form on this trial Portal, it is advisable to continue to submit an item that is required on the main Portal: a list of drawings and documents. This can be used to explain what are the drawings under appeal, and set out how any submissions have been amended over the course of the application. You can upload this as an additional document with the 'Add plan document' button.

Example of what a typical list might read

17 Village Road, London: appeal against refusal of planning permission for rear extension.
List of drawings and documents upon which the LPA made their decision:

- 123-01 Proposed block plan
- 123-02 Rev B Proposed elevations (revision B submitted 12 April)
- 123-03 Rev A Proposed floor plans (revision A submitted 12 April)
- 123-04 Existing floor plans and elevations
- 123-05 Ordnance Survey red line location plan
- Design & Access Statement, by ABC Architecture, dated 15 February
- Flood Risk Assessment, by MNP Flooding, dated 12 February
- Revised Arboricultural Report, by XYZ Trees, dated 9 April
- Daylight report, by EFJ Lighting Ltd, dated 10 April (additional information submitted)

This example imagines the original proposed elevation and floorplan drawings with the planning application were amended during the LPA's determination process, an amendment was made to the tree report, and additional evidence was submitted regarding daylight.

The clear explanation helps the Case Officer at the Inspectorate, and the appointed Planning Inspector, to understand why the planning application form may have referred to different drawing numbers and documents to those uploaded with the appeal. Using these two lists, with a simple explanation of the different drawings and documents, avoids any questions in the Case Officer's mind – and the Inspector's mind – as to whether you have submitted the correct drawings, and what drawing should be considered. As mentioned before, you need to make things easy for the Case Officer and Inspector.

Additional plans

This section is effectively asking for the drawings that were, if relevant, sent to the LPA prior to any amendments being made. So in the example above, it would be the original drawings '123-02 and 123-03'. The detailed list of drawings and documents you produced for the previous section will have explained the status of anything that you upload here.

Other application documents

This section asks you to upload any documents and reports that you submitted to the LPA as part of the planning application. There are drop-down menus to select for each report type, and multiple documents can be uploaded.

The documents you sent to the LPA with the planning application still form part of your case at appeal so it is essential that they are seen, eg any supporting Planning Statement, tree survey, flood risk assessment. The list of drawings and documents that you produced for the 'Plans' section should have set out these supporting documents, with an explanation if any had been amended. There can be many documents and you want the Inspector to know what should be read and, as mentioned, unfortunately sometimes these go astray. This is another reason why, although not asked for on the trial Portal, a clear list should be provided to make sure all documents are seen.

Other submitted documents

This Section allows any other documents to be submitted. If so, ensure it is referenced on your list of drawings and documents.

Site details

The questions in this section ask simple details about the appeal site location, and then continues to ask whether the site can be seen from public land, and if access to the land is restricted. The questions also include whether you consider a site visit is necessary; this is a new question for the Portal, as the Inspectorate will now determine some appeals without a site visit.

These questions are asked for the purposes of the Planning Inspectorate arranging, at a later date, the arrangements for the Inspector to visit the appeal site. You need to consider these questions carefully. The Inspector will need to be able to view everything relevant to the case: the location of the proposed development and anything related to the decision, eg if the reason for refusal may have mentioned effect on trees, then the Inspector will want to see that, or if there is an effect on the windows to nearby houses, the Inspector will want to view those.

If all the features can be seen from public land, and the Inspector does not need to enter the site to undertake any measurements, or check other facts, then there is an advantage in confirming that the site can be seen from public land. Such a site visit is termed an 'Unaccompanied Site Visit' and they are unannounced as the Inspector simply looks at the site from public land. This means the visit may occur sooner since it is easier for the Planning Inspectorate to schedule unaccompanied visits to Inspectors as they do not need to notify parties, and this means they can sometimes be allocated to Inspectors at short notice if, for instance, another case is cancelled.

However, if you want to be certain that the Inspector sees everything on the site relevant to the case you are making, and that cannot be done from private land, then answer the questions in the appropriate way. You need the Inspector to understand the whole case, and so he/she needs to view everything. Also, if the Inspector turns up to an unannounced, unaccompanied site visit and realises that, in fact, there is a need to enter private land then the site visit is likely to be postponed, which will lead to further delay. Such appeals are termed 'Access Required Site Visits', and a specific appointment is made for the Inspector to visit the site.

'You may not necessarily have your choice on the site visit as the LPA area also asked for their opinion and the Inspectorate have the final say (more on this later).

Listed building status

This series of questions determines whether there is a listed building at the appeal site. If there is, then questions are asked regarding the grade of listing, whether listed building consent has been applied for, the outcome of any such application, and if any refusal of consent is being appealed at the same time.

Main grounds of appeal

This is where you set out your case for the appeal. The Full Statement of Case must be submitted with the lodging of the appeal. There is a drop-down menu that provides some guidance on this submission, as well as a definition of 'special category information', which relates to a tick-box question that you need to answer.

Supporting grounds of appeal documents

Any supporting documents, such as appendices to your Statement, can be uploaded here.

Other appeals

This is a straight-forward question regarding whether there are other appeals already lodged on the appeal site. If you click 'Yes' then you are asked to enter the details.

Costs

There is the opportunity for costs to be awarded in planning appeals. It is the only area of the town planning system where there is a punitive costs regime. Costs can be awarded against the LPA, but also against the appellant and third parties. Unreasonable behaviour must be demonstrated, and the intention of the costs regime is to encourage good practice, to ensure that LPAs exercise their duties properly, and that appellants do not pursue unnecessary appeals.

How to apply for costs – and how to avoid having them awarded against you – is discussed in this book. If you wish to apply for costs then there are time limits for that, but it should be indicated at the lodging of the appeal.

Ownership

When the planning application was made to the LPA a certificate would have been completed to list the applicant's interest in the land and, if necessary, to list other owners of the land. A similar certificate is submitted at the time of the appeal which states the ownership of the land on the date of lodging the appeal.

The ownership certificate must be completed correctly or else the appeal might be invalid on receipt. Alternatively, at some point in the future, an owner of the land might be able to claim the appeal was falsely made and seek a legal challenge to the decision. You therefore need to fill in these items correctly. 'Owner' means a person having the freehold interest or a leasehold interest with 7 years or more to run.

This section of the trial Portal leads you through the ownership issue through a series of questions. If you own the whole appeal site and the site is not an agricultural holding, then the questions simply lead you back to the main page again: you have effectively filled out 'Certificate A', which is for when the appellant has been the sole owner of any part of the land to which the appeal relates for the 21 days before lodging the appeal.

If you do not own all of the appeal site but know who does own the other parts, then click 'No' to that question. You are then asked if you have notified all of the site owners. This is what is termed 'Certificate B', and requires you to serve formal notice on all other owners to inform them that you are lodging the appeal. If you fail to do this, then the appeal could be invalid. There is formal wording for this that must be used, which is attached at Appendix 2 of this book. Serving notice should be done in person or by recorded post. The Portal then requires you to upload a list of all the site owners' names and addresses, and the date when Notice was served.

If you do not own all of the appeal site and know some of the owners, but not all, then click the relevant answer. This option means you must serve formal Notice on the known owners in the same manner as with Certificate B. However, you must also publish that same notice in a local newspaper (at your cost), and then fill in what is known as Certificate C. This is so that any other owners may become aware of your intention to appeal. You must send a copy of the published notice to the Planning Inspectorate with your appeal, along with the completed Certificate C, the wording of which can be found online at **www.gov.uk/government/publications/planning-appeal-site-ownership-certificates**

If you do not know the owners of the land then you must publish the same Notice as set out in relation to Certificate B in a local newspaper (at your cost). This is so that any other owners may become aware of your intention to appeal. This is known as Certificate D and then fill in what is known as Certificate D. This, again, is so that any other owners may become aware of your intention to appeal. You must send a copy of the published notice to the Planning Inspectorate with your appeal, along with the completed Certificate D, the wording of which can be found online at **www.gov.uk/government/publications/planning-appeal-site-ownership-certificates**

As with the ownership certificate, when the planning application was made to the LPA, a certificate would have been completed declaring whether the application site was an agricultural holding. The Inspector needs to know this information at the time of the lodging of the appeal, so this is a simple question asking whether the appeal site forms part of an agricultural holding. If no part is an agricultural holding, then you will tick the relevant box and there is nothing else to do. If the site is an agricultural holding, or part of one, and the appellant is the sole agricultural tenant, then you tick the relevant box and there is nothing else to do. However, if there are other agricultural tenants then, when you tick the relevant box, you must serve notice, using the same notices and procedure as set out earlier in relation to Certificate B.

Preferred procedure

There are three choices on the type of procedure, and you can choose which one you would prefer the appeal to follow. These are outlined below, with more detail in this book.

Written Representations

The Written Representations procedure is the quickest and simplest, and is by far the most common as it is suited to most appeals. The process involves the submission of written submissions by the appellant and the LPA. The Inspector visits the appeal site, but determines the appeal solely on the basis of these written documents. In all appeals, except for HAS and CAS appeals, there is a right of reply to these statements for the appellant and LPA, and also the opportunity for third parties, eg neighbours, to write in.

There are advantages in the Written Representations procedure, such as the shorter timeframe and that a well-argued written submission can be very persuasive. But it can lack the opportunity to thoroughly examine the issues through questioning the LPA's refusal, and also the Inspector does not have so wide an interrogative role: they can only read the submissions, and do not ask their own questions.

Hearings

The Hearing procedure takes longer to determine. The process again involves the exchange of written statements and the opportunity for third parties to comment. However, the appeal will see a Hearing which is an informal forum for discussion led by the Inspector, attended by the appellant, the LPA and any other interested parties. This gives a far greater scope for exploring the issues in the case. The Inspector will always visit the site with an accompanied site visit and makes the decision based on everything in the written documentation and said at the Hearing and the site visit.

The advantages of the Hearing route are therefore that there is a greater chance for the Inspector to be aware of the whole case, through submission at the Hearing and by questioning of the appellant and LPA. The disadvantage, as well as the longer time, is that as you are present at the Hearing, the LPA and the Inspector are likely to ask you questions, and not everyone is good at explaining themselves in person and there is a possibility of 'putting your foot in it' with an unfortunate comment during the Hearing; a well-considered written statement can avoid that.

Inquiry

The Inquiry procedure takes longer still. It is a highly formalised process. There is the submission of an appeal statement with the lodging of the appeal, but during the course of the appeal the Planning Inspectorate will inform you when a full Proof of Evidence must be submitted to provide a detailed case. This comes before the date of the Public Inquiry itself: a formal event, similar to a court of law in some respects, where the appellant and the LPA usually have legal representation. This process allows for even greater scope to explore and interrogate the issues in the appeal, and to formally question the LPA about their decision. The Inspector will again visit the site, and make the decision based on all the evidence from the Inquiry and written evidence.

The advantage and disadvantages of the Inquiry are similar to a Hearing, but to a greater extent, ie there is even more possibility to examine the issues, but the appellant's evidence will also be thoroughly tested, probably through formal cross-examination. If legal representation is used, there is also a considerable cost.

What to choose?

The choice of the process is, initially, with the appellant. However, the Planning Inspectorate is not obliged to accept that request, and also the LPA may request a different procedure. The Planning Inspectorate have certain criteria for the procedure; some types of appeal are seen as needing only the simpler processes (the Planning Inspectorate are conscious of the increased resources necessary for the Hearing and Inquiry processes), whilst some types of appeal must always follow the more complex processes (since it is recognised there is a need to interrogate facts). The general guidance is:

- Written Representations appeals are suitable for cases where the grounds of appeal can be understood from written documents, and the issues are not complex, with no need for the Inspector to test evidence through questioning. Refusals of planning permission for householder planning applications, or minor commercial developments, are almost certain to proceed through the Written Representations route, and so go into the HAS or CAS procedure.
- Hearings are appropriate where there is a need for the Inspector to test evidence through questioning, or there is considerable local interest, or the status or personal circumstances of the appellant are at issue (usually agricultural workers' dwellings or traveller sites). There should not be any need for formal questioning by an advocate, or evidence to be on oath.
- Inquiries are appropriate where there are complex issues, or a clear need for evidence to be tested through formal questioning by an advocate, or substantial public interest, or evidence to be tested on oath.

Most appeals follow the written procedure. As can be seen from the above list, it is only where cases are more complex that the Planning Inspectorate is likely to agree to a Hearing, and unless the case falls into the specifics examples of an Inquiry then that process is unlikely. If you select the option of a Hearing or an Inquiry, then the online form will ask you to give the reasons for requesting that route.

This means that if you wish to be heard orally, to make your voice heard in front of an Inspector, you must give the Planning Inspectorate very good reason to allocate a Hearing or Inquiry. It is not good enough just to say in general terms that you want to be heard, but you will need to explain why there is, for example, particular complexities in the case, or a need for evidence to be examined in detail, or a need to question the LPA about certain matters, or there are particular personal issues to be discussed. The Planning Inspectorate case officer will want to know why your case fits within the criteria for a Hearing or Inquiry, and it is up to you to give them that detail.

Technical reports

The purpose of this question, in what is a trial Portal, is not clear, since it seems to ask for information that you would be looking to upload in your 'Main grounds of appeal' submission. But, if you feel you have a technical report that fits better into this category, then upload it here.

Other relevant appeal information

This general question allows you to upload any further documentation you feel should be provided. If you do, then make sure there is a clear explanation as to what it is, and why you are submitting.

There are two matters that are standard questions in the main Appeals Casework Portal that are not on the trial Portal. Therefore, if relevant, you might want to upload at this question the following documentation.

Planning Obligation

Discussions with the LPA during the course of the application may have required you to enter into a legal agreement, or the reasons for refusal set out on the Decision Notice may refer to this. This might be, say, to provide a sum of money for affordable housing, or to limit the use of land in some way. If you agree with the need to provide a legal agreement then it is very important to realise that a dated, signed and executed legal agreement must be in place before the Inspector issues his/her formal decision: many appellants are unaware that planning permission cannot be granted 'subject to' a legal agreement.

Not surprisingly, legal agreements can take a long time to produce. You should therefore be undertaking that work at the earliest opportunity, in consultation with a solicitor, to ensure an agreement is completed. Such a document can be submitted with the lodging of the appeal or during the course of the appeal, provided the Inspector and the LPA have sufficient time to review it. If your case involves a legal agreement then you can upload it here. Or, if it is under preparation but not yet complete, you might have a draft, or Heads of Terms that you want to upload here.

Draft Statement of Common Ground

If you intend to follow the Hearing or Inquiry route then you might wish to send this document, which is a written statement containing factual information about the appealed scheme which you consider will not be disputed by the LPA. The intention of the Statement is that time is spent in the Hearing or Inquiry looking at just the differences between the appellant and the LPA. The draft Statement typically covers:

- Description of the site, including agreed dimensions
- Description of the area
- Planning history of the site

- Development plan policies and supplementary planning
- Agreed data or other factors, eg covering matters such as traffic, trees, ecology, etc.

Plans or drawings relating to the application but not previously seen by the LPA

There is very limited scope to consider revised proposals through the appeal process. It is very important to realise this: the appeal system is not a forum for seeking changes to the refused scheme, in an attempt to try to come to a development that is acceptable to all parties. The system does not have a process to consult with the LPA, neighbours and other parties about any amendments to a development, and so accepting changes might be unfair.

This is a common misconception with appellants, who often attempt to submit amended plans or descriptions of development to address the LPA's reasons for refusal, or else set out a desire to negotiate an agreed solution. It is possibly for this reason that, whilst the option to upload plans not seen by the LPA is a standard question on the main Portal, it has been dropped from the trial Portal.

However, amendments may, exceptionally, be accepted by the Inspector. But in deciding whether or not to accept any changes, the principles of fairness to all parties will be taken. This means that the Inspector will consider whether the changes materially alter the nature of the proposed development, and also whether anyone who would normally have been consulted about a development scheme would be prejudiced by the lack of opportunity to comment on the revised plans.

For example, if an application for a two-storey extension has been refused permission by the LPA on the grounds of the height being so tall as to lead to a loss of light to neighbours and being overbearing to their garden, it is unlikely an amended plan that shows a change to the extension will be accepted by the Inspector. The neighbours may still have their opinions about the size of the amended extension, and the appeal process is not a forum to undertake consultation on this.

But, there may be small matters that could be clarified or modified through amended plans. For instance, if an application for an extension to a commercial property had been refused permission by the LPA on the grounds of harm to a tree, overshadowing neighbours, and that the doors to the new bin storage area opened outwards onto a footpath and blocked pedestrians, then you might be able to submit an amended plan showing a revised access to that bin store. This would not overcome all the issues, of course, but could assist in removing one area of contention at appeal and might well be accepted by the Inspector as it is a minor change that is unlikely to be of much dispute, and solves a simple technical issue.

The key message is that only very minor changes might possibly be accepted by the Inspector, so it is best to steer clear of seeking amendments if possible. However, if you think there is a very minor change that could be overcome, you could upload information here, with an explanation. But it is entirely within the decision of the Inspector as to whether it is accepted.

SUBMITTING YOUR APPEAL

The main screen allows you to complete sections of the form at different times. If you have not fully completed a section, or uploaded the correct documents, then it will show as 'In progress'.

The Planning Inspectorate

Messages My cases Appeals Search My profile Help Logout

Appeal a planning decision

Check your progress

You will only be allowed to submit your appeal when all the sections below have been completed

Open to appeal [illegible] | **148 days left**

1. About the planning application

Planning application details	COMPLETED
Environmental details	IN PROGRESS
Plans	IN PROGRESS
Additional Plans	IN PROGRESS
Other applications documents	IN PROGRESS
Other submitted documents	IN PROGRESS

2. About the site

Site details	COMPLETED
Listed building status	COMPLETED

3. About the appeal

Main grounds of appeal	IN PROGRESS
Supporting grounds of appeal documents	IN PROGRESS
Other appeals	IN PROGRESS
Costs	COMPLETED
Ownership	IN PROGRESS
Preferred procedure	IN PROGRESS
Technical reports	IN PROGRESS
Other relevant appeal information	IN PROGRESS

4. About You

Contact details	IN PROGRESS

5. Submit the appeal

Check your answers	IN PROGRESS

It is only once you have completed all sections that you will be able to formally submit the appeal. Once you have lodged the appeal to the Planning Inspectorate you will soon receive an email that has two pdf attachments which are the appeal form and the personal details form. These will now have a unique reference number on them (starting 'APP'), which is your appeal reference. The top of the forms will also have a time and date stamp that confirms the date you submitted the appeal to the Inspectorate.

SEND A COPY OF THE APPEAL TO THE LPA

You are required to send a copy of the appeal to the LPA straight away. This means both the pdf appeal forms you have received from the Inspectorate and a copy of your Appeal Statement with any supporting documents. In lodging the appeal you have made a formal declaration that you will do this, and it is an important part of the procedure. No reminder is sent, so it is very important you do this immediately. Each LPA has a different email address, and these can be found at:

www.gov.uk/government/publications/sending-a-copy-of-the-appeal-form-to-the-council

KEY POINTS

- Don't miss the deadlines for an appeal. You will lose your right of appeal if you do!
- Take time to gather all the documents necessary before lodging the appeal: the application documents and your appeal documents. You don't want to be rushing around at the last minute trying to find key items.
- Check and double check the documents you intend to upload are the complete ones. If the Case Officer finds at a later date you have missed an item, and you are past the appeal deadline, you may lose your right of appeal.
- Think carefully about the procedure you want to follow: Written Representations, Hearing or Inquiry. You have a choice, but if you want a Hearing or Inquiry you need to provide good reasons to the Inspectorate.
- The Case Officers at the Inspectorate, and the Inspectors themselves, like clear and comprehensive lists of documents. Even though the trial Portal does not ask for it, use lists to set out what drawings and documents you submitted with the planning application, and what drawings and documents were actually refused permission by the LPA.
- You cannot amend a refused scheme through the appeal process or enter into negotiations.
- Don't forget to send a copy of the appeal to the LPA.

Appendix 2: Ownership certificates

OWNERSHIP CERTIFICATES

When you lodge an appeal you are required to inform the Planning Inspectorate who owns the appeal site. If the land is not entirely within your ownership then you must serve Notice on any owners you know and, if there are any you do not know, publish a Notice in the local newspaper.

The following pages have the wording of the two relevant Notices. You should use one or the other as appropriate:

- Notice of planning appeal
- Notice of CAS appeal

If you also need Certificates C and D (see Chapter 4 and Appendix 1), these can be found online at **www.gov.uk/government/publications/planning-appeal-site-ownership-certificates**

For planning appeals (except CAS) the wording is:

Town and Country Planning (Development Management Procedure) (England) Order 2015

Notice under Articles 13 and 36 of the Town and Country Planning (to be published in a newspaper and where relevant, on a website or to be served on an owner* or tenant**)

Proposed development at (a)..

....

I give notice that (b)..
having applied to the (c)...
Council to (d)..is
appealing to the Secretary of State
against the decision of the Council +
or the failure of the Council to give notice of a decision +

Any owner* of the land or tenant** who wishes to make representations about this appeal should write to

The Planning Inspectorate
Temple Quay House
2 The Square
Bristol
BS1 6PN

By (e)...

If you decide to make representations you should make it clear that you are an owner of the appeal site or tenant of an agricultural holding on the site and you should give the site address.

*"owner" means a person having a freehold interest or a leasehold interest the unexpired term of which is not less than seven years, or in the case of development consisting of the winning or working of minerals, a person entitled to an interest in a mineral in the land (other than oil, gas, coal, gold or silver).

**"tenant" means a tenant of an agricultural holder any part of which is comprised in the land.

Signed ....

On behalf of.. *(delete if not applicable)*

Date.......................

Statement of owners' rights

The grant of planning permission does not affect owners' rights to retain or dispose of their property, unless there is some provision to the contrary in an agreement or in a lease.

Statement of agricultural tenants' rights

The grant of planning permission for non-agricultural development may affect agricultural tenants' security of tenure.

+delete where inappropriate

Insert (a) address or location of the proposed development
(b) applicant's name
(c) name of the Council
(d) description of the proposed development
(e) date giving a period of 21 days beginning with the date of service, or 14 days beginning with the date of publication, of the notice (as the case may be)

For CAS appeals the wording is:

Town and Country Planning (Development Management Procedure) (England) Order 2015

NOTICE OF APPEAL UNDER ARTICLES 13 AND 36
(to be served on an owner* or a tenant** in the case of an appeal against the refusal to grant planning permission for minor commercial development***)

Proposed minor commercial development*** at (a)..

I give notice that (b) ....having applied to the (c)...Council to (d) ....
....is appealing to the Secretary of State against the refusal of the Council to grant planning permission for the proposed development.

In the event that the appeal is dealt with by the expedited procedure under the Written Representations procedure+, any representations made by the owner* of the land or tenant** to the Council about the application will be passed to the Secretary of State and there will be no opportunity to make further representations in relation to the appeal.

* "owner" means a person having a freehold interest or a leasehold interest the unexpired term of which is not less than 7 years.

** "tenant" means a tenant of an agricultural holding any part of which is comprised in the land.

*** "minor commercial development" means development of an existing building, or part of a building, in use for certain commercial purposes. It does not include a change of use, development not wholly at ground floor level, an increase in floor space or a change to the number of units in a building.

+ The expedited procedures in relation to Written Representations are set out in Part 1 of the Town and Country Planning (Appeals) (Written Representations Procedure) (England) Regulations 2009 (S.I. 2009/452).

Signed..

On behalf of (delete if not applicable).........................

Date ....

Statement of owners' rights

The grant of planning permission does not affect owners' rights to retain or dispose of their property, unless there is some provision to the contrary in an agreement or in a lease.

Statement of agricultural tenants' rights

The grant of planning permission for non-agricultural development may affect agricultural tenants' security of tenure.

Insert:

(a) address or location of the proposed development
(b) applicant's name
(c) name of the Council
(d) description of the proposed development

Glossary

Commercial Appeals Service (CAS)
A planning appeal for small commercial developments, which runs under the Planning Inspectorate's fast-track programme.

Conservation Area
An area of land that is designated by an LPA as being of special architectural or historic interest, whose character or appearance they wish to preserve or enhance. A designated area of land can vary in size and by what type of land, water or buildings are covered.

Costs
The ability for one party to pay another party's costs in the appeal process. However, unlike the courts, an award of costs does not automatically follow an appeal decision and can only be made if there has been unreasonable behaviour by one party.

Decision Notice
The formal decision by an LPA on a planning application that grants permission or refuses permission.

Delegated Report
The detailed report on a planning application that is written by the planning case officer.

Development plan
The plan produced by an LPA that sets out policies against which any development proposal will be judged, and which will also be considered by the Inspector in the determination of the appeal. It may comprise a number of adopted documents, including local plans, neighbourhood plans and spatial strategies.

Dwelling and Dwellinghouse
A dwelling is a self-contained building or part of a building used as a residential accommodation, and usually housing a single household. A dwelling may be a house, bungalow, flat, maisonette or converted farm building. Certain parts of planning legislation have specific interpretations for the terms with, in particular, flats being specifically excluded from the definition of a 'dwellinghouse'.

Final comments
The stage during a planning appeal where the appellant has the right of reply to the LPA's appeal statement and any submissions by third parties.

Hearing
The route for a planning appeal which involves the exchange of written submissions and then an informal Hearing session chaired by the Planning Inspector, which allows for a discussion of the appeal.

Heritage asset
A building, monument, site, place, area or landscape identified as having a degree of significance meriting consideration in planning decisions because of its heritage interest. This may include assets designated by bodies such as Historic England, eg listed buildings, and also those identified by the LPA, eg locally listed buildings.

Householder Appeals Service (HAS)
A planning appeal for extensions and alterations to single family houses, which runs under the Planning Inspectorate's fast-track programme.

Inquiry
The route for a planning appeal which involves the exchange of written submissions, the submitting of Proofs of Evidence, and then a formal Inquiry with the Planning Inspector and usually legal representation.

Legal agreement

An agreement entered under s106 of the Town and Country Planning Act 1990 to mitigate the impacts of a development proposal. Can also be called a planning obligation, a Unilateral Undertaking, or a s106 agreement, depending on the format of the agreement.

Legal challenge

The only way to change the decision of an Inspector, through the High Court.

Listed building

A building that has been identified for its special architectural or historic interest. Works to that building are the subject of additional protection and needs consent under the Planning (Listed Buildings and Conservation Act) 1990, but the LPA must also have regard to development that affects the setting of a listed building.

Local Plan

See Development plan.

LPA

Abbreviation for local planning authority, which is the public authority which undertakes the planning authority for a particular area. This is typically the district, borough or metropolitan council, but will include, in various parts of the country, the county council, Broads Authority, National Park Authority, the Mayor of London or a development corporation.

National Planning Policy Framework (NPPF)

The Government's policy on planning, which can be a material consideration in all planning decisions undertaken by an LPA.

Non-determination appeal

An appeal lodged following the failure of the LPA to determine a planning application within the statutory timescale.

Ownership certificates
The certificates that must be completed with the lodging of the appeal that confirm the ownership of the appeal site; a similar certificate will have been completed at the planning application stage. An agricultural holdings certificate must also be completed confirming if any land is part of a holding.

Planning conditions
Wording that may be attached to a grant of planning permission typically to regulate or restrict the approved development, or requires the submission of additional information, or to clarify the terms of the permission. They must meet the tests of necessity and relevance, must be precise, enforceable and reasonable, and there is a right of appeal against conditions.

Planning Committee Report
The detailed report on a planning application that is written by the planning case officer for the purposes of the relevant Committee of the LPA. It will usually set out a recommendation to approve or refuse planning permission, with the final decision made by the Members of that Committee.

Planning Inspector
A person appointed by the Secretary of State for Housing, Communities and Local Government to determine a planning appeal.

Planning Inspectorate
The Government agency that runs the planning appeal system. Liaison between appellants, LPAs and third parties is with an allocated case officer at the Planning Inspectorate.

Planning Practice Guidance
The Government's guidance on specific planning issues, including heritage, noise, trees, flooding.

Representation
A general term for any submissions made by main parties, or third parties, to a planning application or appeal. It is a neutral term, as representations may be made in support or opposition.

Site visit
The visit to the site by the Inspector, either through an Unaccompanied Site Visit (which is viewing only from public land) or an Access Required Site Visit (where the Inspector will enter the appeal site).

Statutory period
The time period within which an LPA must determine the planning application.

Supplementary Planning Document (SPD)
A document produced by the LPA which adds further detail to the policies in the development plan, eg guidance for development on specific sites, or on particular issues such as design. Supplementary planning documents (SPDs) can be a material consideration in planning decisions but are not part of the development plan.

Third parties
A person, or group, who has an interest in a planning application or appeal who is not one of the main two parties: the LPA and the applicant/appellant.

Written Representations
The route for a planning appeal which involves the exchange of written submissions, followed by the Inspector's site visit.

Printed in Great Britain
by Amazon

18466197R00093